D1186921

036829

LANDSCAPE CONSTRUCTION
VOLUME 2

LANDSCAPE CONSTRUCTION
VOLUME 2

Roads, Paving and Drainage

C. A. Fortlage and E. T. Phillips

Gower

Published by
Gower Publishing Limited
Gower House
Croft Road
Aldershot
Hampshire GU11 3HR
England

Gower
Old Post Road
Brookfield
Vermont 05036
USA

British Library Cataloguing in Publication Data
Fortlage, C. A. (Catharine A.)
 Landscape construction
 Vol. 2: Roads, paving and drainage
 1. Roads – Design and construction 2. Pavements – Design and
 construction
 I. Title II. Phillips, Elizabeth, 1930– III. Roads, paving and
 drainage
 625.7

ISBN 0 566 09042 2

Library of Congress Cataloging-in-Publication Data
Fortlage, C.A. (Catharine A.)
  Landscape construction / C.A. Fortlage, Elizabeth Phillips.
  v. <1 > : ill. : 25 cm.
  Includes bibliographical references and index.
  Contents: v. 1. Wells, fences, and railings.
  ISBN 0–566–09041–4
  1. Garden structures—Design and construction. I. Phillips,
 Elizabeth (Elizabeth Thelma) II. Title.
 TH4961.F67   1992
 624—dc20   91–28570
                                                                   r91

Typeset in Great Britain by Bournemouth Colour Press Limited, Parkstone, Dorset and printed in Great Britain at Bourne Press Ltd, Bournemouth.

CONTENTS

TABLES

FIGURES

PLATES

FOREWORD

Landscape is becoming of increasing importance to both urban and rural developments, but sadly many good landscape designs are marred by the unfortunate detailing of the hard landscape. When completed this series will provide the first comprehensive work on construction written specifically for the landscape designer who, until now, has had to rely on extracts from technical information, manufacturers' catalogues, British Standards and architectural textbooks for information.

The three volumes of *Landscape Construction* will cover all aspects of hard landscape building and construction work. Basic building construction is an essential part of the training and professional skills of the landscape designer, and these texts will fulfil the need for straightforward and clearly illustrated information on each subject. There are plentiful illustrations supplemented by photographs on all aspects of hard landscape.

The first volume covered the principles of construction of brick and stone landscape walls, fences, security barriers, gates, and railings, together with their fittings and finishes. This second volume covers monolithic, unit and granular paving, kerbs, edgings, light road construction and drainage. The third volume will cover services, light structures, earth and water retaining structures and will include a section on construction failures and remedial work.

Together the three volumes of *Landscape Construction* will be an essential desktop reference work for the landscape designer who is concerned with good standards of construction and workmanship; and they should do much to give the student of landscape design a sound technical foundation for his professional work.

Professor Derek Lovejoy
MA(Harvard) DipTP FRIBA FRTPI PPILA FRSA FIHT

INTRODUCTION TO VOLUME 2

This book covers the construction of hard paved surfaces which can be used for roads, paths or open areas; it does not deal with the construction of full-scale highways, as these are not within the landscape designer's province.

Roads are intended either to take the swiftest route to their destination, or to follow a serpentine route in order to create an impression of spaciousness or to display landscaped vistas to the traveller. The Romans brought with them their expertise in making long-lasting roads and pathways, and indeed many of the smoothest and sturdiest roads today are laid on Roman foundations. The techniques of Roman road construction could usefully be studied by the landscape designer today, in particular the careful construction of the base, the bedding of the pavement stones, and the falls and cross-falls which ensured a stable road.

Paths likewise can either take a direct route or be designed to provide an attractive perambulation in a detailed landscape. They may also be used in intriguing patterns such as mazes or labyrinths. Paths can be gentle, unconstrained guides to wandering through an informal landscape, or they can be designed to direct people firmly in a chosen direction. It is only recently that paths have been paved; earlier pavements were merely part of the road since the traffic was slow enough to be dodged, and routes across country were just tracks on the natural ground since all except the 'carriage folk' wore good solid boots or went barefoot. Moreover, horses prefer to travel on soft ground rather than paving, so that during the centuries of horse transport there was no demand for paved horseways, though wagons had to be provided with hard roads.

The paved open space for public assemblies started in Europe with the Greek agora (hence agoraphobic = fear of open spaces) and was followed by the Roman forum. Both these areas were intended for the use of free citizens only, who took part in government, and not for the meeting of peasants or slaves. After the collapse of the Roman system of government, the populace were not encouraged to meet in large numbers which might be seen as a protest against feudal power, so the urban open space degenerated into a market place for the sale of livestock. The neo-classic layout of open spaces in large cities was intended for ceremonial parades, public announcements, executions, and other manifestations of government power. With the exception of public gatherings to celebrate great events such as Coronations and the Cup Final, the modern urban open paved area seems to have little purpose except that of an overflow car park. Landscape designers need to use all their imaginative skills to create an interesting and purposeful open space.

Monolithic paving (that is, liquid or semi-liquid paving laid as a sheet surface) was not known until the nineteenth century and until that time most country roads were made of broken stone while town roads were cobbled. Paved areas in towns were made of cobbles, bricks, granite, or hardwood (usually elm) setts and most had greater falls and steeper cambers than modern paving. What is now considered 'quaint' and a great tourist attraction was and still is a practical solution to the drainage of these areas; it is only the car and bus which demand very flat surfaces which are liable to ponding in heavy rain. Large paving units such as Caithness or York stone, some as large as small doors, were reserved for strategic positions. Country roads were maintained by roadmenders who sat by the roadside breaking large stones brought from the quarry into fist-sized pieces which were placed in the ruts and compacted by the iron-tyred carts. Turnpikes (where a toll was levied) were usually well maintained, but where the repairs were the responsibility of a parsimonious parish authority they were often in a deplorable state.

After the Romans departed, properly constructed roads and paved areas were not common until McAdam developed a method of laying the road material in several compacted layers on a carefully prepared base, thus enabling the coaches of the nineteenth century to achieve their remarkable time-keeping records. A later development was the introduction of tar-McAdam, a tar-bound surface which became the standard paving material until the introduction of bituminous materials and asphalt. The base varied according to the type of sub-strate and its ability to drain; in areas of clay for example greater falls, steeper cambers and drainage ditches at each side were needed to prevent flooding and muddying of the road. The design of modern roads is a highly complex business, beyond the scope of the ordinary landscape contract, but even simple pedestrian and light vehicle paths and roads need careful construction if they are to stand up to their intended usage.

1   H<small>ARD LANDSCAPE</small> S<small>URFACES</small>

Hard landscape surfaces may be divided into three main types: monolithic, unit and granular. In this book the term 'paving' is used for pedestrian areas, footpaths and playgrounds, while the term 'roadway' is used for hard surfaces carrying traffic such as hard standings, lightly trafficked private roads and car parks, though the distinction between the two types is not precise. Heavy duty road construction is outside the scope of this book, as it is the concern of the highway engineer, and should such work come within the scope of a landscape contract, it will not be something that landscape designers will tackle themselves, though they may have to allow for heavy delivery lorries and access for engineering plant in their part of the design. Sturdy paving is an essential component of any landscape design, as landscape maintenance is becoming ever more mechanized, and where the traditional hand mower would cause little damage crossing a paved area, a modern tractor and gang mower may cause severe scarring and cracking unless the paving is designed to take their weight and abrasion. As public bodies are now obliged to use contract services, there is much less control over the workers on the site, and nothing but a stout barrier will prevent contractors taking the shortest way to the job, even if it is across 'pedestrian only' paving. It is therefore very important that the landscape designer should be able to specify the right type of paving for the job, and be aware of the effect of a particular type of paving on the design. Typical examples are given in Figure 1.1.

Monolithic paving

Monolithic paving is laid as a continuous sheet of material, and includes road 'carpets' such as tarmacadam (now little used), asphalt, bitumen macadam and in-situ concrete.

Monolithic paving can be laid comparatively quickly; this means that the final coat can be laid clean and undamaged at the end of the contract without delaying the handover. Monolithic paving is also usually cheaper to construct than unit

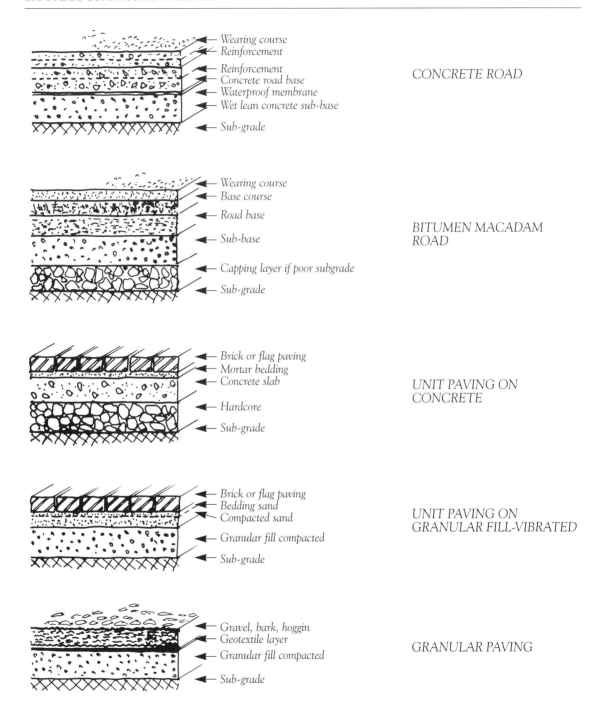

Figure 1.1   Typical paving construction

paving, and litter collection and cleaning can be done by machinery, as there are no edges and ridges to trap refuse or water. The surface is not as attractive as unit paving, since, apart from expansion and division strips, patterns are limited to surface texturing. Ribbing, studding, or other types of pattern can be impressed on the surface when the material is still flexible. The available colours and textures are limited, bitumen macadam being black or red, and although concrete can be coloured, the range of colours is small and the rather monotonous uniform colour is not particularly attractive. Coloured concrete can be laid in bays, strips, or squares to form patterns. This section deals with the surfaces laid by ordinary contactors, while the special monolithic sports surfaces used for artificial outdoor pitches are briefly described in this book, but as they are mostly supplied and laid by specialist contractors, the details of their construction and materials tend to be a matter of commercial secrecy.

Unit paving

The term unit paving comprises ordinary bricks, special paving bricks, paviors, paving tiles, rectangular paving blocks, interlocking blocks, cobbles set in concrete, concrete or stone setts, stone flags, precast concrete flags and grass concrete blocks. Unit paving offers the landscape designer the widest possible range of prices, sizes, textures and colours, ranging from the economical plain concrete flag used for city pavements to the very expensive natural slate or Yorkshire stone flags. Unit paving is often chosen by landscape designers for its appearance rather than for its performance. The very wide range available, together with the potential for interesting pattern making, makes unit paving the best choice where the landscape designer wishes to use paving as an important element in the design (see Figure 1.1 and Figures 3.1 to 3.9).

Unit paving can be laid in small and complicated areas such as internal courtyards and shopping malls, especially where the paving is designed to lead smoothly from the outside to the inside of the building, as most unit paving is equally satisfactory externally and internally. It is admirable for paving which adjoins buildings, as the small scale and bonded patterns are in harmony with brick or stone walls, thereby helping to 'settle' the building on the ground. Buildings sitting on mass concrete or bitumen macadam look abruptly detached from their surroundings. Unless the paving base is soundly constructed, even slight settlement will cause some units to sink or rise, leaving sharp edged 'trippers' for the careless or unsteady pedestrian. This hazard frequently occurs when paving is relaid after lifting and replacing units for maintenance or repair of underlying services, and individual units may be fractured by impact or frost with the same result. It is not always possible to obtain exactly the same paving as the original when repairs have to be carried out, and in heavily used public areas where damage and wear are probable, the landscape designer would be well advised to choose a fairly ordinary type of unit paving which is likely to remain in production for some time. British Standard precast concrete flags are stocked by most builders' merchants nationwide; admittedly they are not very interesting in appearance, but they are reliable in quality and easily available. Many types of unit paving, in particular ordinary bricks and natural stone flags are not resistant to oil or other stains, and should not be specified where spills and staining are likely to occur. The strong cleaning chemicals available do more harm than good to most paving materials, even if the deterioration does not show immediately; where remedial cleaning has to be carried out the advice of both the paving supplier and the chemicals' supplier should be obtained.

Granular paving

Granular paving includes loose gravel, bound gravel, hoggin, shale (or blaes), cobbles laid loose, reinforced soil, shingle, ballast, bark and wood chips, chippings and quarry scalpings (the broken remains left after stone block removal).

These paving materials are used mainly for rural or domestic pedestrian paths; some are suitable for bridleways but they are not suitable for any areas where vehicle overrun is likely to occur regularly. Granular paving is very flexible on slopes and changes of angle; it absorbs settlement and frost-heave without permanent damage, and its appearance is not spoilt by minor scarring and scraping. In the main it consists of natural materials whose colour range is limited to tones of brown, buff, cream and grey which harmonize well with soft informal landscaping. Artificially coloured materials are available but the colours tend to be very strong and very uniform, and are more suited to interior landscaping and graveyard decoration than to outdoor landscaping. Maintenance and repair are cheap and simple; raking, weed control, and digging out and replacing badly damaged areas are all that is required apart from occasional top dressing with the same material. Granular paving does not withstand vehicles or constant and heavy pedestrian traffic, and is prone to nourish weeds. It is liable to be displaced by kicking and running; and though the softer materials absorb stains well it is not easy to clean litter from the surface of them. Most granular materials must have the support of edge restraint both during construction and permanently to prevent the material dispersing over the surrounding ground. Loose cobbles, shingle or heavy ballast must never be used in public areas; they are too useful as ready made ammunition for vandals and rioters apart from being great litter traps, so that any landscape designer who specifies such materials in inner city areas must expect to receive claims for all the broken car and house windows in the neighbourhood. There are disadvantages in the looser forms of granular paving (such as pea gravel) on sloping pathways subject to heavy rain, as the loose particles have the unfortunate habit of rolling to the foot of the slope every time a storm occurs, and the luckless owner can spend many hours raking it all up to the top again ready for the next storm.

Safety of paving surfaces

The *Construction, Design and Management Regulations* came into force on 31 March 1995, and it is now critical that the landscape designer specifies materials fit for their purpose. On completion of the contract it is advisable to give the client a Comissioning Document describing the uses for which the paving was designed and the maintenance requirements of all surfaces. For paving of all types the landscape designer should check the slip resistance of the surface with the manufacturer before choosing a particular product, and preferably get a written statement of the tested slip resistance. The slip resistance of a wet paving surface is much lower than that of a dry surface, and figures for both wet and dry conditions must be obtained. If there are accidents (even a long time after the paving has been laid) the landscape designer will be in line for the blame, but if it can be shown that the paving as laid had a slip resistance adequate for the intended use, it may be possible to avoid claims for compensation.

1.1 BASES FOR PAVING AND ROADWAYS

Unless landscape designers choose to specialize in the design and construction of roads and pavements, it is unlikely that they will be responsible for any but the most lightly trafficked areas. Roads and paved areas such as industrial yards carrying continuous heavy traffic are the province of civil engineers or road engineers. However, any integrated design involving estate roads, car parks, loading bays or pedestrianized areas is likely to include landscape design, and it is important to be able to discuss these elements sympathetically and intelligently with the engineers and understand their problems as well. The terminology used is to a great extent unique to roads, though unfortunately both terminology and specifications vary in technical standards, specifications and guidance notes on the subject. The glossary below has attempted to rationalize these terms and make them useful to student and practitioner alike. These terms will then be discussed in detail in the relevant sections, together with the method of using them in worked examples.

Meaning of road construction terms

- *California Bearing Ratio* (CBR): the expected loading on a road given as a percentage; a higher percentage gives a better bearing ratio. (The origin of the term 'California Bearing Ratio' is hidden in the mists of time and the archives of the Road Research Laboratory.) CBR figures are given in Table 1.3.
- *Carpet*: common name for the final layer of the surface; usually applied to a monolithic finish.
- *Cement Bound Material* (CBM): aggregate and cement compacted to form a sub-base or road base.
- *Channellized traffic*: traffic which wears the roadway into definite 'tramlines', usually heavy goods vehicles running in a narrow roadway.
- *DoT Spec*: Department of Transport Specification for Highway Works. This is the highway engineer's 360 page 'bible'; the current issue is dated 1986 and

has a whole booklet dated 1988 devoted to revisions.

- *Fall*: the slope of the road surface along its length; 'crossfall' is the fall across the width from one side to the other; 'camber' is the fall from the centre to both sides. Falls are given either in percentages, degrees, or ratios. The formulae for changing one to the other are:

Change angle to percentage:

$$\frac{90}{\text{angle}} = Z \text{ then } \frac{100}{Z} = X\%$$

Change ratio to percentage:

$$1:\text{length} = \frac{1}{\text{length}} = X\%$$

- *Finish*: the top surface and its immediate bedding material, usually applied to unit paving.
- *Formation level*: the natural or improved ground level on which the road or paving is formed.
- *Geotextile filter membrane*: a fine flexible fabric which allows water to pass through, but prevents fine soil particles from being squeezed up into the sub-base and damaging its stability.
- Granular materials: Department of Transport Type 1 and Type 2; these are carefully graded aggregate mixes which will compact into a firm sub-base or bedding.
- *Paving*: in this book the term refers to unit and granular paving whether for a private drive, pedestrian area or footway.
- *Plasticity index*: a measure of the difference in the moisture content of a soil between the state of being too liquid or too dry to be plastic.
- *Road base*: levelling layer above the sub-base; the term applies mainly to monolithic construction.
- *Standard axles*: a notional factor used in the method of calculating the expected flow of traffic over the economic life of the road or paving.
- *Sub-base*: the main structural and levelling layer of the roadway or paving on which the stability of the construction depends.
- *Sub-grade*: the natural or engineered ground level (also known as sub-strate).
- *Sub-strate*: the preferred name for sub-grade.
- *Sub-strate improvement*: may be required where the sub-strate performance as a foundation for a roadway or paving requires upgrading.
- *Wet lean concrete*: a weak mix of concrete below normal structural strength used for the sub-base of monolithic roadways.

Road classes for the landscape designer

The following five classes of roads and pavements have been devised by the authors to enable the landscape designer to distinguish between the types of construction needed for different purposes. For any more complicated road or paving construction, it will be wise to hand the work over to a highway engineer or at least to discuss the work.

Class A: Pedestrian only roadways and paving

Hard paved areas with no vehicular access. These include footways, cycle paths and pedestrian areas separated from roads by bollards or similar barriers to prevent vehicle overrun. Wherever footways and pedestrian only areas are designed and constructed as Class A roads or pavements, it cannot be stressed too strongly that unless they are cut off by bollards or similar obstructions, vehicle overrun and unlawful parking will cause damage to both kerb and finish and destroy the beauty of the design. Class A roadways and paving can be quite lightly constructed, but beware, as there may be a requirement for access by emergency and maintenance vehicles (any of which can be large, high and heavy); in this case a full road specification must be used over the whole area, or the vehicle access and routes restricted. Either way, a DoT Category 1 roadway as described below will be required.

Class B: Occasional traffic

Small private car parks, driveways, pedestrian areas and cycle paths with occasional emergency and maintenance vehicles moving freely over the area.

Class C: Lightly trafficked roads

These are DoT Category 1 roadways, and include non-through residential roads, public car parks and delivery areas for light vans.

Class D: Regular trafficked roads

These are DoT Category 2 roadways which carry up to 75 commercial vehicles per day in each direction, they include superstore access roads.

Class E: Heavy duty roadways

These comprise bus stations and warehouse access roadways and loading bays which have to deal with the continual movement of heavy vehicles; because of their continual slewing and braking they cause more stress and point loads than normal and therefore require a heavier specification.

Design of sub-bases

Although the sub-base of most pedestrian landscape paving does not need much design calculation, there may be occasions when the landscape designer must be involved in the design of lightly trafficked areas. The calculations for heavily trafficked areas require accurate site and laboratory investigation of soil types and bearing capacities, and unless the landscape designer is qualified to deal with such problems, the work must be left to a highway engineer. It is necessary to determine several site factors and the expected traffic before calculations can be made; these are described below.

Soil classification

Soils are classified for sub-base purposes into six types and two categories according to the level of the water table, and they are given a CBR rating number expressed as a percentage. The accurate measurement of the CBR should be carried out in accordance with the procedure given in Clause 7 of BS 1377: Part 4, which is rather too long and complicated to be included in a book on basic construction, but a simplified table for a range of soil types is given in the Calculations of Sub-base Thicknesses (see pages 12–14).

Plasticity index

The plasticity index is a measure of the difference in the moisture content of a soil between the state of being too liquid to be plastic, and the state of being too dry to be plastic. Thus heavy clay has a wide span of moisture content while still being plastic, whereas the moisture content of sand has a very small span. These figures apply to consistent soils on fairly level ground; it is important to appreciate that particularly wet or dry conditions may distort the CBR findings. In order to use the figures given in Table 1.3 the landscape designer must determine the actual condition of the site as well as the type of soil.

Geotextile filter membranes

In areas with a high water table, or where there is a very fine soft sub-grade, the landscape designer should consider including a 'geotextile filter membrane' between the sub-grade and the sub-base. This is a fine flexible fabric which allows water to pass through, but prevents fine soil particles from being squeezed up into the sub-base and damaging its stability. Geotextile filter material is made in various thicknesses and densities which allow the passage of varying amounts of water. The manufacturer should be consulted to decide which type is appropriate for the given site conditions.

Preparation for sub-base

Before the sub-base is laid, a certain amount of preparation must be done or else the sub-base will not be stable.

All tree roots in the sub-soil should be cut back well clear of the paved area; it may also be desirable to treat the sub-soil with a total herbicide if there is any likelihood of persistent weed seeds being present. Where there are patches of loose soil, extra damp areas, recent fill, old drains, or any other break in the continuity of the sub-grade, these areas should be dug out and replaced with well-rammed hardcore laid in layers not more than 150 mm thick, or granular material to match the strength of the main sub-grade soil type as far as possible. It is better practice, though not always feasible, to scrape out poor sub-strate material rather than to dig it, as digging may loosen the sub-strate and make bad ground worse. After this has been done, the whole of the sub-grade should be rolled with a 2.5 tonne roller, or hand compacted with a mechanical rammer. It may be necessary to 'blind' the sub-grade with sand or ash if the material is so open as to allow the bedding material to fall into it. The finished sub-grade should not vary more than 10 mm from the final paving profile, otherwise the bedding material will be too thick or too thin, with consequent uneven settlement.

The sub-base must be designed to remain in good condition for the life of the paving, and one way of ensuring this is to deal with any water retained in the sub-grade or sub-base. The sub-grade may be a naturally free-draining soil such as gravel or coarse sand, but if it is water-retentive such as clay, land drainage should be installed, since continual water percolation loosens the soil structure and allows it to deform. The sub-base must also drain freely if the paving is not to become waterlogged with the risk of freezing and spalling or of lifting the paving units. At the low points in the sub-grade (or in the sub-base if the sub-grade is naturally free-draining), filter-wrapped perforated plastic or clay agricultural drains should be laid, connected to a soakaway or the site land drainage system. The drain trench should be backfilled with granular material, consolidated (but not rammed) to match the strength of the sub-base. A minimum overall depth of 450 mm is necessary to prevent frost from penetrating the ground and causing frost-heave in the paving; the omission of this precaution is the reason why so many gates cannot be opened wide in frosty weather. The drainage and disposal of surface and ground water is described in greater detail in Chapter 6, Drainage of paved areas.

Sub-grade (or sub-strate)

This is the starting point for the roadway construction, which has to be strong enough to take the traffic load; it is measured as the California Bearing Ratio (CBR). Sub-grade levels should have an ideal tolerance of ± 25 mm in the specified levels, but this is unlikely to be achieved in practice. If the natural soil is a good consolidated gravel, all is well, and it only needs to be rolled with an 8–10 tonne roller to consolidate it fully before the next layer is laid. Where the natural soil is unstable or is made of fill, or contains organic material, the weak spots must be cut out by hand (not by digger) and filled with granular material. For a reliable road which will not end up as a mountain bike test track it is best to use aggregates complying with DoT granular fill Type 1 for this purpose. DoT granular fill Type 2 can be used for lightly trafficked roads if it is quite certain that the client will not decide to buy 44 tonne articulated lorries the day after the road has been laid. Both types of fill must comply with clause 803 or 804 of the *Department of Transport Specification for Highway Works*, but in practice Type 2 is rarely used. Table 1.1 shows the drainage capability of various soils and their suitability for road foundations.

Sub-base edges

These are constructed before the sub-base material is laid, since it must be properly compacted right up to the edge. If there is to be a permanent kerb this can be laid

Table 1.1
Permeability of soils

Soil type	Drainage	Frost risk	Use as road foundation
Boulders and cobbles	good	very slight	good – excellent
Hardcore			
broken stone, brick	excellent	very slight	very good – excellent
chalk, soft rock	fair – poor	medium – high	good – excellent
Gravel			
well graded (no fines)	excellent	none – very slight	excellent
with fines	fair – poor	slight – medium	good – excellent
Sand			
well graded (no fines)	excellent	none – very slight	good – excellent
with fines	fair – poor	slight – high	fair – good
Silt	poor	medium – high	poor – fair
Clay			
low plasticity	very poor	medium – high	poor – fair
moderate plasticity	fair – bad	slight	poor
high plasticity	bad	very slight	bad – poor
Peat	fair – poor	slight	very bad

first, or if the edges are to merge into soft landscape, steel road formers can be used. These are reusable steel strips made to various profiles which hold the road material in position until it has set. They are then removed leaving the road edge to blend into the soft landscape.

Sub-base materials
The sub-base is the main layer of material which is used to form a sound structural foundation for the roadway or paving, and to adjust the levels and gradients, and its construction is critical. For light traffic loading and pedestrian areas a DoT Type 1 or 2 granular sub-base is satisfactory. For regular traffic loading the sub-base can be made of 'wet lean concrete' which is very weak concrete with less cement content than structural concrete. The most commonly used sub-base is made of 'cement bound material' (CBM) such as hardcore, gravel, hoggin, brick-earth, or broken stone, hard brick or concrete bound together with cement. CBM made with less satisfactory materials such as clay and sand can be used with more cement, but such materials should not be used except for very lightly trafficked areas.

Granular sub-base
A granular sub-base should consist of aggregate to the specification of DoT Type 1 or Type 2 to Clause 803 or 804, and are identified as:

● Clause 803 granular sub-base material Type 1 must be crushed rock, crushed slag, crushed concrete or well burnt non-plastic shale graded from 75 mm to

75 μm. (Only Type 1 may be used for heavily trafficked roads.)
- Clause 804 granular sub-base material Type 2 must be natural sands, gravels, crushed rock, crushed slag, crushed concrete or well burnt non-plastic shale graded from 75 mm to 75 μm but in different proportions to Type 1.

All these materials must pass a 75 mm sieve, and they must be free from dust or any pollutant such as oil or other chemicals. The thickness of the granular sub-base depends on the type of soil and the load which the paving must carry. Major roads are designed by highway engineers who must calculate the number and frequency of vehicles using the road in order to arrive at the thickness of the sub-base, but for most landscape work the figures given in this book are adequate. Where heavy lorries are likely to use the paving regularly, the landscape designer is advised to consult a highway engineer, as the calculations are somewhat complex.

Wet lean concrete
Sub-bases or road bases can be made of 'wet lean concrete' which has less cement, and can be specified in four grades equivalent in strength to the Cement Bound Material grades CBM 1, CBM 2, CBM 3 and CBM 4. The grades of concrete for sub-bases are specified in *DoT Specification for Highway Works*, Clauses 1001 to 1006. Table 1.2 shows the comparative strengths of these materials.

Table 1.2 Comparative strengths of road base materials		
Type	Concrete mix to BS 5328: Part 1	Equivalent CBM grade
wet lean concrete 1	ST 1 (previously C7.5, C7.5P)	CBM 1
wet lean concrete 2	ST 2 (previously C10, C10P)	CBM 2
wet lean concrete 3	ST 3 (previously C15, C15P	CBM 3
wet lean concrete 4	ST 4 (previously C20, C20P)	CBM 4

Cement bound material (CBM)
Although the landscape designer is not likely to be involved with critical road design – this can thankfully be left to the highway engineer – it may be useful to know what the various types of CBM are in order to choose the most economical specification. Cement bound materials are classified in the DoT specification as CBM 1, CBM 2, CBM 3 and CBM 4 according to their strength.

- CBM 1 has very carefully graded aggregate from 5.0–75 μm, with a 7-day strength of 4.5N/mm^2.
- CBM 2 is the same range of aggregate but with more tolerance in each size of aggregate with a 7-day strength of 7.0N/mm^2.

- CBM 3 must be crushed natural aggregate or blastfurnace slag, graded from 5.0 mm–150 μm for 40 mm aggregate, and from 20–75 μm for 20 mm aggregate, with a 7-day strength of 10N/mm².
- CBM 4 must be crushed natural aggregate or blastfurnace slag, graded from 5.0 mm–150 μm for 40 mm aggregate, and from 20–75 μm for 20 mm aggregate, with a 7-day strength of 15N/mm².

Any CBM with an aggregate:cement ratio larger than 24:1 should not be used except for the lightest of hard standings with very little traffic. If pfa (pulverized fuel ash) is used together with Portland cement the CBM will be stronger. This type of sub-base consists of clean hard aggregate material, at least 15 per cent of which passes a 75 mm sieve, bound with cement and laid in situ; the material is then compacted by vibrating rollers. Several light passes give better compaction than one heavy roller pass. CBM can be laid in situ if the existing sub-grade is gravel; the water and cement are then churned carefully and accurately into the gravel and compacted to produce the sub-base. Alternatively the CBM can be mixed in a concrete mixing plant in the usual way. The sub-base should be rolled with an 8–10 tonne roller not more than two hours after mixing and laying, and it must be cured for seven days before the road base or surfacing is laid, while if an open textured material is used the surface should be blinded with coarse sand. If frost-heave is likely the sub-base should be 300 mm minimum thickness. Cement bound material sub-bases are more suitable for large areas of paving not subject to heavy loading such as urban pedestrian areas or lightly trafficked estate roads.

Calculation of sub-base thickness

Step 1: Determine the expected volume of traffic
This is rated as a number of 'standard axles' and is calculated by taking the actual number of commercial vehicles expected to use the road or pavement, and then multiplying this by a given factor to get a notional number expressing the number of 'standard' axles. The factors are:

- Roads with less than 250 commercial vehicles per day: multiply by 0.45
- Roads with 250 to 1000 commercial vehicles per day: multiply by 0.72

(Where vehicles 'track' with their wheels following the same line every time, as happens in very narrow one-way roads or turning circles, the number of standard axles should be multiplied by 2 or even 3 to give a true loading factor. Remember that heavy vehicles cause more damage than light ones (one 10 tonne truck = 16 five tonne trucks).

Step 2. Find the CBR for the soil type

Table 1.3
California Bearing Ratios for soil types and construction conditions

Soil type	Plasticity index	High water table 300 mm or less below formation level			Low water table 1000 mm or more below formation level		
		Construction conditions					
		poor (%)	average (%)	good (%)	poor (%)	average (%)	good (%)
Heavy clay	70	1.5–2.0	2.0	2.0	1.5–2.0	2.0	2.0–2.5
	60	1.5–2.0	2.0	2.0–2.5	1.5–2.0	2.0	2.0–2.5
	50	1.5–2.0	2.0–2.5	2.0–2.5	2.0	2.0–2.5	2.0–2.5
	40	2.0–2.5	2.5–3.0	2.5–3.0	2.5	3.0	3.0–3.5
Silty clay	30	2.5–3.5	3.0–4.0	3.5–5.0	3.0–3.5	4.0	4.0–6.0
Sandy clay	20	2.5–4.0	4.0–5.0	4.5–7.0	3.0–4.0	5.0–6.0	6.0–8.0
	10	2.5–3.5	3.0–6.0	3.5–7.0	2.5–4.0	4.5–7.0	7.0 or >
Silt	—	1.0	1.0	2.0	1.0	2.0	2.0
Sand: unevenly graded	—	20.0	20.0	20.0	20.0	20.0	20.0
evenly graded		40.0	40.0	40.0	40.0	40.0	40.0
Sandy gravel: evenly graded	—	60.0	60.0	60.0	60.0	60.0	60.0

Notes:
1. High water table is commensurate with ineffective sub-soil drainage.
2. All the figures in columns under construction conditions are percentages.

Step 3: Determine the sub-base thickness required
This should be done according to the CBR (California Bearing Ratio) from Table 1.4.

Table 1.4
Minimum sub-base thicknesses

CBR	Standard axles						
	20,000	40,000	60,000	80,000	100,000	200,000	400,000
	(mm)	(mm)	(mm)	(mm)	(mm)	(mm)	(mm)
under 2%	510	520	530	530	540	560	570
2%	360	370	380	380	390	410	420
3%	270	280	290	290	290	310	320
4%	200	210	220	220	230	240	260
5%	160	170	180	180	190	200	210
6%	120	130	140	140	140	150	160
7%	100	100	100	110	110	120	130

In practice, 150 mm is the minimum sub-base thickness where the sub-base has been 'improved', or where the sub-grade material is as good as Type 1 granular material. In all other cases 200 mm is the minimum if the sub-base is laid directly on the sub-strate. This is due to the following factors:

- The figures given in Table 1.4 are intended for the construction of highways, where the grading is most carefully carried out and consolidated; there are three or even four layers of bases below the surface finish; and there are lots of supervising engineers.
- It is not really feasible to lay exactly 100 mm or 110 mm of granular material on site; the JCB or excavator levelling the sub-base cannot be controlled to that accuracy, nor can granular fill dumped from a truck be laid so carefully.
- The Standard Method of Measurement (SMM7) used for calculating the cost of the contract only recognizes changes in thickness of 100 mm in filling with granular material. There is therefore no cost advantage in trying to squeeze the last 10 mm off the minimum thickness of sub-base required for a particular paving system.

An example of this design procedure is shown for a superstore delivery roadway:

Number of lorries expected per day	= 50	
Multiply by working days per year	= 50 × 312 days	= 15,600 vehicles
Multiply by assumed life of roadway	= 15,600 × 20 years	= 312,000 vehicles
Convert to standard axles	= 312,000 × 0.45	= 140,400 s.a.

The sub-grade is sandy clay with a low water table, plasticity index of 20, and the site conditions are good. The CBR is therefore between 4.5 per cent and 7 per cent. The paving system chosen is 80 mm blocks on 50 mm sand bed, with a CBR of 4.5 per cent. By interpolation, the table gives a sub-base of 200 mm.

The landscape designer should note that these calculations do not make any allowance for changes in traffic density or type of vehicle; such variables are the responsibility of the client, who must be held accountable for traffic forecasts over the economic life of the road or pavement.

Simplified calculation

When the CBR rating of the soil has been determined, the thickness of the sub-base may be calculated from Table 1.5, which is based on the *Department of Transport Specification for Highway Works*, an extremely complicated document dealing with the construction of highways which may prove interesting to those landscape designers who have become bored with competition crosswords, higher mathematics and chess problems. The figures in Table 1.5 are rule-of-thumb thicknesses which are useful for estimating, but more exact calculations should be used for the design of paving systems for areas carrying vehicular traffic. The classes are those described on pages 6–7.

Table 1.5
Thickness of sub-bases for road classes A to C

CBR %	Class **A**: footways, patios, garden paths, house parking (mm)	Class **B**: pedestrian areas, occasional vehicle overrun (mm)	Class **C**: car parks, minor roadways with no through traffic (mm)
Under 2%	380	500	550
2%	230	350	400
3%	180	260	300
4%	160	200	230
5%	140	160	190
6%	120	120	140
7% and over	100	100	100

1.2 CONCRETE

Concrete in one form or another comes into most hard landscape design, sometimes as a base for other materials, sometimes as a substitute for natural stone, and sometimes as a decorative material in coloured or textured patterns. The names and mixes of concrete keep changing all the time, and while the architect and engineer need to specify concrete in great detail for structural purposes, unfortunate landscape designers have to follow their British Standard specifications even when they only want to fill in round a manhole cover. There is no harm in specifying the proper grade of concrete for a particular job, even if only to cover the landscape designer's rear elevation. This section gives a short explanation of some terms used in concrete specification to enable the landscape designer to choose the best mix for the purpose.

Concrete grades

Concrete specification is described in BS 5328: Parts 1 and 2, in which concrete is classified by grades defining its strength at 28 days after laying; this strength is expressed in N/mm^2. The exposure to which the concrete is subjected affects the grade to be specified (see Table 1.6).

Non-structural concrete for landscape work in 'mild' or 'moderate' conditions has no minimum grade requirement. There are standard concrete grades lower than C20 which are suitable for non-structural landscape work:

C7.5 strength 7.5 N/mm^2 C10 strength 10.0 N/mm^2 C15 strength 15.0 N/mm^2

15

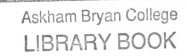

Table 1.6
Exposure classification for structural concrete

Condition	Type of exposure	Minimum grade	28 day strength
Mild			
	surfaces protected against weather	unreinforced C20	20 N/mm²
	or aggressive conditions	reinforced C30	30 N/mm²
Moderate			
	exposed but sheltered from severe rain	unreinforced C30	30 N/mm²
	or freezing when wet	reinforced C35	35 N/mm²
	concrete under non-aggressive water		
	concrete in contact with		
	non-aggressive soil		
	concrete subject to condensation		
Severe			
	exposed to severe rain, alternate	unreinforced C35	35 N/mm²
	wetting and drying, occasional	reinforced C40	40 N/mm²
	freezing, severe condensation		
Very severe			
	occasionally exposed to seawater	unreinforced C40	40 N/mm²
	or de-icing salts	reinforced C40	40 N/mm²
Most severe			
	frequently exposed to seawater	unreinforced C45	45 N/mm²
	or de-icing salts, or in tidal zone	reinforced C50	50 N/mm²
Abrasive			
	exposed to abrasive action	unreinforced C45	45 N/mm²
	by machinery or grit	reinforced C45	45 N/mm²

Concrete mixes

There are four ways of specifying a concrete mix: as a designed mix, a prescribed mix, a standard mix, or a designated mix. Standard and designated mixes will probably be the landscape designer's choice for simple hard landscape construction.

Designed mix

The purchaser specifies the performance required of the concrete; the producer is then responsible for selecting an appropriate mix. Strength testing is essential for compliance with the specification. Designed mixes should be used where strength is important, and the concrete grade is included in the specification of the mix as a check on the strength of the concrete.

Specifying a designed mix is quite complicated as there are many items to be decided by the specifier and this exercise should only be undertaken when a designed mix is essential. This is unlikely to happen in a landscape contract, but if it should be necessary, the specification must include:

- concrete grade
- size of aggregate;
- permitted type of aggregate;
- permitted type of cement;
- minimum cement content;
- maximum water:cement ratio;
- workability (slump);
- quality assurance required.

Prescribed mix

The purchaser specifies the constituents of the concrete and is responsible for ensuring that the concrete will meet the performance requirements. The assessment of the mix proportions (but not strength) is essential for compliance with the specification. The specification for a prescribed mix must include:

- type and strength class of cement;
- size of aggregate;
- permitted type of aggregate;
- proportions of each component of the concrete mix;
- workability;
- quality assurance required.

Standard mix

The mix is selected from the restricted list given in BS 5328: Part 2: 1991 s.4 and is made with a restricted range of materials. The assessment of the mix proportions (but not strength) is essential for compliance with the specification. The specifier must tell the producer what the concrete is going to be used for, and the specification for a standard mix must include:

- standard mix reference;
- permitted type of cement;
- size of aggregate;
- permitted type of aggregate;
- workability;
- quality assurance required.

These items can only be chosen from the standard lists given in Tables 4 and 5 in BS 5328: Part 2: 1991.

Designated mix

The mix is specified in BS 5328: Part 2: 1991 s.5 and requires the producer to hold current product conformity certification with quality approval to BS EN ISO 9001.

17

Quality assurance is essential for compliance with the specification. Designated mixes should only be used where quality assurance is reliable. These mixes are not open to variations by the specifier and are chosen by considering their applications rather than by the make-up of the concrete.

Most concrete for small scale and landscape work is specified either as designated mixes or standard mixes. Older documents may refer to different names for mixes, and these are shown in brackets alongside the Standard mixes. Some recommended mixes for typical landscape applications are shown in Table 1.7.

Table 1.7
Recommended concrete mixes for typical landscape applications

Application	Standard mix	Designated mix	Slump (mm)
mass concrete fill	ST 1 (C7.5P)	GEN 1	75
or	ST 2 (C10P)		
mass concrete foundations in:			
non-aggressive soils	ST 4 (C20P)	GEN 4	75
mild sulphate soils	—	FND 2	75
bad sulphate soils	—	FND 3	75
very bad sulphate soils	—	FND 4	75
kerb bedding and haunching	ST 1 (C7.5P)	GEN 1	10
drain pipe support	ST 3 (C15P)	GEN 3	10
in-situ concrete paving:			
pedestrian or light vehicle	—	PAV 1	75
heavy vehicle	—	PAV 2	50

Workability

An important property of fresh concrete is its 'workability' as concrete which must flow round reinforcement must be more workable than concrete to be laid in a plain slab. Workability depends on the amount of water in the mix, and this is checked on site by a 'slump test' which consists of putting a sample of concrete in a special slump cone and measuring the drop when the concrete slumps after the cone is lifted off. The wetter the concrete the greater the slump.

Traditional concrete mixes

When dealing with very small jobs, probably using unskilled labour mixing its own concrete in a bucket on site, the names of the traditional mixes may prove more intelligible: these are given in Table 1.8.

Table 1.8
Traditional names of concrete mixes and applications

Application	Traditional name of mix	Cement:aggregate:sand (parts by volume)	
Setting posts, filling weak spots in ground, backfilling pipe trenches ('all-in' is mixed aggregate as dug from the pit)	one, two, three one to five all-in	1:2:3 1:5	or
Paving bases, bedding manholes, setting kerbs and edgings, setting precast channels	one, two, four one to six all in	1:2:4 1:6	or
In situ concrete paving	one, one&half, two&half	1:1.5:2.5	

2 MONOLITHIC PAVING

Monolithic paving is laid as a continuous sheet, in the form of a hot or cold semi-liquid material. This chapter covers monolithic paving for macadam and asphalt roadways, and in situ concrete paving. These materials are generally cheaper than unit paving, as they are laid mechanically rather than manually, and they are best suited to large open areas where appearance is of less importance than cost and durability. This book does not deal with the construction of highways, as the design of the structure, gradients, loading, drainage and surfacing of these roads is a highly skilled job and must be carried out by a highway engineer and specialist contractors. The monolithic paving in landscape contracts is usually confined to car parks, driveways, access roads on private land, and other trafficked areas which do not come under the Highway Acts. These Acts control the construction, dimensions, lighting and signing of public roads, and although the landscape designer does not normally have to comply with these, it is advisable to design private roadways with those standards in mind. In particular, drainage, lighting and road humps should be up to public road standards as inadequate lighting, icy surfaces and dangerous humps can lead to accidents and consequent litigation. A large part of a hard landscape contract deals with hard surfaces where traffic may or may not go, or where it goes illegally, and therefore the term 'roadway' used in this chapter includes surfaces intended for pedestrians only, as well as all areas where regular or occasional traffic is expected.

Advantages

The advantages of monolithic paving are rapid construction, low cost compared with unit paving, and a degree of flexibility which allows the material to be laid round angles, slopes and corners which would be difficult to lay satisfactorily with unit paving. It may seem unlikely, but monolithic surfaces are easier to repair than unit paving, since the shape and depth of the hole to be patched does not matter, while paving units must be carefully fitted into the existing pattern, nor is it always possible to get a perfect match with the existing units or to achieve perfect workmanship. Slight humps and dips in monolithic paving can be graded into the adjoining surface, whereas a change in level in unit paving creates sharp tripping edges.

Disadvantages

The disadvantages of traditional monolithic paving are: dull appearance, limited choice of colours and texture, and a public assumption that cars are rightfully entitled to go onto any surface which looks like a road. Examples of more enlightened use of monolithic paving can be found in Japan and other countries. While rapid machine laying is an advantage in large areas, hand laying of monolithic paving in small areas is expensive and not always satisfactory, since most monolithic materials need to be compacted to a degree not easily obtained with manual techniques.

2.1 MACADAM ROADWAYS AND PEDESTRIAN AREAS

These are often described as 'tarmac', 'asphalt' or 'macadam' surfaces, but all commonly used road mixes are mixtures of various types of bitumen and aggregate in different proportions. There is a wide range of bituminous mixes available for different purposes. The choice of mixture depends on soil type and traffic loading; wet clay soil needs a stronger paving mixture than well drained gravels, and heavy vehicles cause more damage than light ones. There are four types of bituminous mixtures normally used for road or paving construction:

1. Coated macadam, which is a more open textured mixture using softer bitumen and evenly graded aggregate. This is the main material used for roads of all kinds, and it is often roughened by rolling chippings into the surface to give a better grip.
   Grouted macadam is 40 mm aggregate with a bituminous binder or a mortar of Portland cement and sand, poured after the aggregate is laid.
   Dry coated (or dry bound) macadam is 40 mm aggregate with fine material vibrated into it with an 8–10 tonne vibrating roller to give finished thickness not less than 100 mm.
   Wet-mix macadam is 40 mm aggregate bound with bituminous material.
   Water-bound macadam is 40 mm aggregate bound with fine sand and water.
2. Hot rolled asphalt, which is a close graded mixture using hard bitumen and aggregate with small and large sizes but not many intermediate sizes. Asphalt produces a smoother surface than macadam and is therefore very useful for wheelchair paths, trolley areas and cycle paths. Natural asphalt is little used today, as the mining of the mineral is expensive.
3. Mastic asphalt is a softer and finer material which is used mostly for balconies, roof decks and non-trafficked small areas. It is composed of fine and coarse aggregate and 'asphaltic cement' which forms a cohesive impermeable material, solid or semi-solid, which can be hand laid without compaction.
4. Traditional tars are rarely used as they were a product of coal-gas manufacture which has been superseded by natural gas.

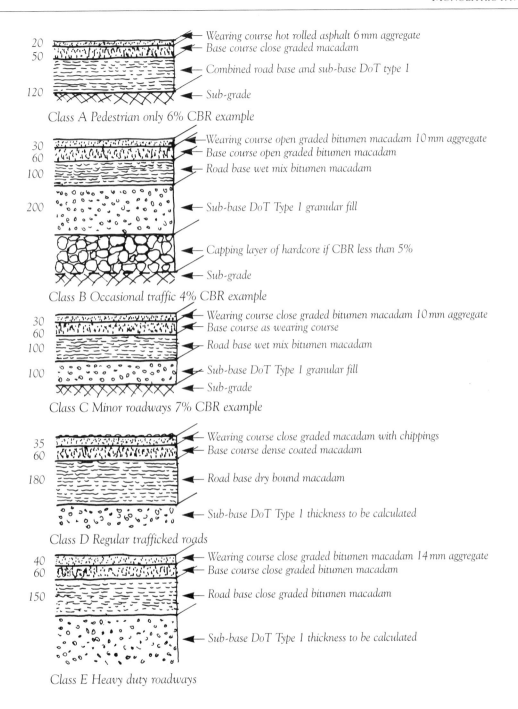

20 — Wearing course hot rolled asphalt 6 mm aggregate
50 — Base course close graded macadam
— Combined road base and sub-base DoT type 1
120 — Sub-grade

Class A Pedestrian only 6% CBR example

30 — Wearing course open graded bitumen macadam 10 mm aggregate
60 — Base course open graded bitumen macadam
100 — Road base wet mix bitumen macadam

200 — Sub-base DoT Type 1 granular fill

— Capping layer of hardcore if CBR less than 5%

— Sub-grade

Class B Occasional traffic 4% CBR example

30 — Wearing course close graded bitumen macadam 10 mm aggregate
60 — Base course as wearing course
100 — Road base wet mix bitumen macadam
100 — Sub-base DoT Type 1 granular fill
— Sub-grade

Class C Minor roadways 7% CBR example

35 — Wearing course close graded macadam with chippings
60 — Base course dense coated macadam

180 — Road base dry bound macadam

— Sub-base DoT Type 1 thickness to be calculated

Class D Regular trafficked roads

40 — Wearing course close graded bitumen macadam 14 mm aggregate
60 — Base course close graded bitumen macadam

150 — Road base close graded bitumen macadam

— Sub-base DoT Type 1 thickness to be calculated

Class E Heavy duty roadways

Figure 2.1   Macadam and asphalt: typical construction

A roadway constructed of bituminous material comprises a sub-base, road base, base course and wearing course.

Sub-base

The construction of the sub-base for macadam roads is described in Section 1.1 Bases for Roadways and Paving (pages 5–15). Sub-bases or road bases can be made of 'wet lean concrete' specified in four grades equivalent in strength to the Cement Bound Macadam grades CBM 1, CBM 2, CBM 3, and CBM 4. The grades of concrete for these layers and the wearing course are specified in detail in DoT Specification for Highway Works, Clauses 1001 to 1006. The maximum size of aggregate permitted for road work is 40 mm, while the strength of the wearing course should be not less than 48.2 N/mm^2, which allows for deviations in mixing and laying. Old names for concrete mixes are shown in brackets in Table 2.1

Table 2.1
Concrete mixes for road construction

Roadway layer	Concrete mix to BS 5328: Part 1
Sub-base or road base:	
wet lean concrete 1	ST 1 (C7.5, C7.5P)
wet lean concrete 2	ST 2 (C10, C10P)
wet lean concrete 3	ST 3 (C15, C15P)
wet lean concrete 4	ST 4 (C20, C20P)
Road base:	
continuously reinforced:	C40
Wearing course (surface slab):	
unreinforced	C40
jointed reinforced	C40
continuously reinforced	C40

The road base

This is the main structural road layer; its thickness is determined by the expected traffic loading and the CBR of the sub-strate. This layer is usually made of dry coated macadam or CBM, but it can be made of dry hardcore only for very lightly trafficked areas, though this is not recommended as more surfacing will be needed in compensation. Either dry coated macadam or wet-mix macadam can be used. A 'tack coat' of soft bitumen must be spread on the sub-base to make a good bond with the final surfacing unless this is laid immediately afterwards.

The surfacing

This layer can be laid in two courses; a base course followed by a wearing course which carries the traffic. This is the final layer of the road which also contributes to the strength of the road. The base course can be made of cheaper materials than the wearing course, which must be resistant to weather, skidding and abrasion. It is usually made of close graded macadam or hot rolled asphalt, while coated chippings can be added to give better grip and abrasion resistance. The bitumen in the coating wears off slightly, leaving the chippings minutely proud of the surface; this gives a good grip but creates a lot of tyre noise compared with smoother surfaces.

Typical roadway outline specifications

The sub-bases for all Classes should be calculated by means of the procedure given on p. 12 or selected from Table 1.5.

Class A: Pedestrian only roadways and paving (see p. 7)

These are hard paved areas with no vehicular access and are more simply constructed than roadways. However, where vehicles regularly cross the footway a full road specification must be used. Footways usually comprise the sub-strate, a base (combined sub-base and road base), a base course and a wearing course. The specification is as follows:

- Sub-strate: as for full scale road but rolled with 2.5 tonne roller. Tolerance ± 20 mm.
- Base: as for sub-base of full scale road. 75 mm thick Roll with 2.5 tonne roller
- Base course: hot rolled asphalt
  or close graded coated macadam
  or open graded coated macadam 20 mm aggregate 50 mm thick
- Wearing course: hot rolled asphalt 6 mm aggregate
  or fine graded macadam
  or medium graded coated macadam
  or close graded bitumen macadam 20 mm thick

Open graded and fine graded bitumen macadams are only suitable for footways and pedestrian areas, as they are less skid-resistant than the coarser surfaces.

Class B: Occasional traffic (see p. 7)

Examples are small private car parks, driveways, pedestrian areas and cycle paths with occasional access for emergency and maintenance vehicles. These roadways may be constructed with the following specification:

- Sub-strate: see section on Bases
- Sub-base :   see section on Bases
- Road base: wet-mix bitumen macadam   100 mm thick
- Base course: open graded bitumen macadam   60 mm thick
  - or   single course bitumen macadam   75 mm thick
- Wearing course: fine graded bitumen macadam   20 mm thick
  - or   6 mm medium graded bitumen macadam   20 mm thick
  - or   6 mm close graded bitumen macadam   25 mm thick
  - or   10 mm open graded bitumen macadam   30 mm thick

Class C: Lightly trafficked roads (see p. 7)

These are DoT Category 1 roadways, and include non-through residential roads, public car parks and delivery areas for light vans. These roadways may be constructed as follows:

- Sub-strate: see section on Bases
- Sub-base: see section on Bases
- Road base: wet-mix bitumen macadam   150 mm thick
  - or   close graded bitumen macadam   100 mm thick
- Base course: close graded bitumen macadam   60 mm thick
  - or   hot rolled asphalt   60 mm thick
- Wearing course: hot rolled asphalt   35 mm thick
  - or   10 mm close graded bitumen macadam   30 mm thick
  - or   6 mm close graded bitumen macadam   25 mm thick

Class D: Regular trafficked roads (see p. 7)

These are DoT Category 2 roadways which carry up to 75 commercial vehicles per day in each direction, including superstore access roads. These roadways may be constructed as follows:

- Sub-strate: see section on Bases
- Sub-base: see section on Bases
- Road base: hot rolled asphalt   135 mm thick
  - or   close graded bitumen macadam   135 mm thick
  - or   dry-bound macadam   180 mm thick
- Base course: dense coated macadam   60 mm thick
- Wearing course: hot rolled asphalt   40 mm thick
  - or   close graded bitumen macadam   35 mm thick

Class E: Heavy duty roadways (see p. 7)

These comprise bus stations and warehouse access roadways and loading bays which have to deal with the continual movement of heavy vehicles. These roadways may be constructed as follows:

- Sub-strate: see section on Bases
- Sub-base :   see section on Bases
- Road base: wet-mix bitumen macadam   200 mm thick
  - or   close graded bitumen macadam   150 mm thick
  - or   hot rolled asphalt   125 mm thick
- Base course: close graded bitumen macadam   60 mm thick
  - or   hot rolled asphalt   60 mm thick
- Wearing course: hot rolled asphalt   50 mm thick
  - or   14 mm close graded bitumen macadam   40 mm thick
  - or   14 mm close graded tar surfacing   40 mm thick
  - or   14 mm mastic asphalt surfacing   35 mm thick
          (mastic asphalt is laid manually and is more expensive)

The overall thickness of the road construction in lorry parking bays should be 650–425 mm for clay sub-grades, 425–350 mm for loam sub-grades and 350–300 mm for gravel sub-grades, but where lorries with point load jacks or heavy steel ramps are working, it may be advisable to include steel reinforcement in the road construction and to increase the thickness of the sub-base. Where a slip-

Plate 1   *Preparations for laying a bitumen macadam roadway: note the size of the equipment required.*

27

Plate 2   *A road train in operation laying a macadam road. Each piece of equipment must be coordinated with the others, and a regular delivery of fresh material is essential. This illustration shows that such a scale of roadway construction is not feasible for small constricted areas.*

resistant surface is vital, such as ramped approaches to sites where pedestrians could be at risk from slipping vehicles, a surface of resin binder with fine calcined bauxite aggregate can be applied, but this is very expensive and can only be justified if the risk of skidding is not acceptable.

Remember that emergency vehicles have to go anywhere at any time, and even if a light surfacing is specified, the road base and sub-base must be strong enough to take emergency vehicles without subsiding, at least until the last casualty has been removed.

Macadam materials

Bitumen
This is the binder used to bond aggregate in the construction of asphalt and coated bitumen macadam for road construction; there are three major sources:

Plate 3 *Macadam surfaces must be laid and rolled at the right temperature and consistency. This is even more critical for hot rolled asphalt, and the contractor must ensure that the site is absolutely ready for macadam or asphalt road works.*

- Bitumen derived from crude oil (most commonly used) and including 'penetration' or hard bitumen, 'cut-back' bitumen which is thinned down, and bitumen 'emulsion' which is a liquid.
- Road tar from distillate of coke production (not much used). Tar mixtures are used where a lot of oil spills are expected, as bitumen can soften with oil, with black and sticky consequences.
- Natural bitumen from Trinidad (now expensive, used only on special work).

Coated macadam
Coated macadam is specified in great detail in BS 4987: Part 1. It is the road material used most often for roads of all types. It is laid hot and is composed of:

- A binder: petroleum bitumen, cut-back bitumen, road tar, or a mixture of tar and bitumen (treated as bitumen).
- Fine aggregate: crushed hard rock or flint, sand, or sand and fines mixed, the material to be under 3.35 mm.

- An added filler: any of the above passing 75 per cent of 3.35 mm sieve, Portland cement, or hydrated lime.
- Coarse aggregate: crushed hard rock such as granite, basalt, limestone, gritstone, or gabbro; gravel of hard rock; blastfurnace or steel slag. The material is accurately graded in standard proportions of each size from the maximum size specified in each type down to 3.35 mm.

Aggregates for macadam

The aggregates recommended for road bases and wearing courses are the following:

- Dense road base:
    40 mm aggregate graded;
    28 mm aggregate graded thickness 70–100 mm.
- Open graded base course: 20 mm aggregate graded thickness 45–75 mm (this is for light traffic only).
- Single combined wearing course and base course: 40 mm aggregate graded thickness 75–105 mm with a minimum thickness of 80 mm if it is used without a separate wearing course.
- Dense base course:
    40 mm aggregate graded thickness 95–140 mm;
    20 mm aggregate graded thickness 50–80 mm.
- Open graded wearing course:
    14 mm aggregate graded thickness 40–55 mm;
    10 mm aggregate graded thickness 30–35 mm.
    (These are the traditional 'carpets' for lightly trafficked roads and need dressing about every two years; they can be coated with bituminous grit to improve tyre grip. This is the stuff that sticks to car tyres, windscreens, and bicycles and fills the drains up.)
- Close graded wearing course:
    14 mm aggregate graded thickness 40–55 mm;
    10 mm aggregate graded thickness 30–35 mm.
    (These are better than open graded for heavier traffic.)
    6 mm aggregate graded thickness 20–25mm.
    (This is a suitable surfacing for estate roads, playgrounds, and footways.)
- Medium graded wearing course: 6 mm aggregate graded thickness 20–25 mm.
    (This is only for light traffic, footways, playgrounds and cycle paths.)
- Fine graded wearing course: 3 mm aggregate thickness 15–25 mm. (This is for urban footways, courtyards, light car parking, footways – use coated chippings on roadways.)
- Pervious wearing course:
    20 mm aggregate graded thickness 45–60 mm;
    10 mm aggregate graded thickness 30–35 mm.
    (This is used for fast traffic where water must drain rapidly to the side of the

road and therefore a steeper camber is necessary. An impermeable sub-strate is necessary to direct the water away from the surface.)

Laying macadam

When laying macadam roads the following criteria must be applied:

- Variations in level from sub-base to road base should be +10 or –30 mm.
- Variations in level from road base to base course should be ±15 mm.
- Variations in level from base course to wearing course for playgrounds, private car parks, and cycle paths should be ±10 mm, and for roads ±6 mm.
- Straight crossfall (from one side to the other in narrow paths), and the camber from crown to channel (centre of roadway to gutter) not less than 2 per cent (1:50) or more than 3 per cent (1:33), with a fall in the channel of not less than 0.8 per cent (1:125).
- Joints should be offset not less than 300 mm from joints in layers below.
- No laying in frost or on ice or snow, or on wet surface. Hand laying of odd corners can be done alongside machine laying.
- Where macadam has to stick to walls or kerbs, these should be coated with hot bitumen or cold thixotropic bitumen before laying macadam.
- Use 6 tonne to 12 tonne rollers for roads, 2.5 tonne rollers for footpaths and playgrounds. Rolling to be done at British Standard specified temperatures – minimum 60°C.

Laying macadam on existing paving

When laying macadam on existing paving the following criteria must be applied:

- New macadam on concrete slab; clean and fill cracks and joints.
- New macadam on sett or block paving; cut out weak spots and fill with concrete or asphalt base course material, rake joints to a depth of 15 mm (hardly practicable with the vast number of joints?), the surface to be tack coated with bitumen emulsion before laying macadam.
- New macadam on old surfaces generally; use tack coat of bitumen emulsion.

Decorative macadam

Although plain dull grey-black macadam is normally specified, there may be occasions when a variation in colour is desirable, either for demarcating special areas or as an essential part of the landscape design. There are three possible ways of obtaining a decorative effect: by using a coloured macadam, by surfacing with an ornamental aggregate, or by dressing the surface with a textured material.

Coloured macadam can be produced in two ways; either by adding a pigment to the hot mix and using a coloured aggregate, or by using a coloured aggregate only. The colour of the aggregate will not show until the thin layer of bitumen over it is worn off, but the coloured mix gives an immediate effect, though the tone is never very bright. New macadam mixes are made in lighter colours which compare well with coloured concrete. More expensive are the clear resin binders manufactured by specialist firms, which allow the true colour of the aggregate to be seen. These surfaces comply with the British Standard for bitumen macadam, but they are mixed and laid by specialist firms. This enables the landscape designer to use light coloured aggregates which look less like a road than the ordinary black macadam, and therefore are less likely to encourage illegal parking, but naturally they will show oil and tyre marks more than black bitumen compounds. They look very attractive for roadways and paths round old buildings, and in other conservation work.

Surfacing the macadam with a coloured aggregate rolled into the wearing course is a method only suitable for very lightly trafficked areas, as tyre rubber and oil soon spoil the appearance of heavily trafficked roads. Only fine graded asphalt and fine graded macadam are capable of bonding aggregate on the surface, and the aggregate should be pre-coated with clear resin to give a good bond.

Textured macadam is produced by applying a fine coat of bitumen emulsion or tar spray and rolling in decorative chippings; it is not hardwearing and the chippings are liable to come adrift even in normal use, but it is satisfactory for areas where only pedestrian traffic is expected.

2.2 ASPHALT

Asphalt is specified as 'hot rolled asphalt'. Not surprisingly, it is laid hot and rolled at certain critical temperatures which enable it to be spread evenly. Road asphalt nowadays is nearly always a man-made bituminous compound, though traditionally lake asphalt from Trinidad was used. It is made of various proportions of the following materials:

- Binder: bitumen or lake-asphalt bitumen.
- Fine aggregate: fines under 2.36 mm of hard rock or flint, sand, or sand and fines mixed.
- Added filler: very finely ground limestone or Portland cement.
- Coarse aggregate: material graded in standard proportions of each size from the maximum specified in each type down to 2.36 mm, composed of crushed hard rock such as granite, basalt, limestone, gritstone or gabbro; gravel of hard rock; blastfurnace slag or steel slag.

The description of these ingredients makes it clear that asphalt is a finer and more expensive material than coated macadam, and the landscape designer should only use it where it is really necessary. The relevant British Standard is BS 594: Part 1, and the standard specifies a great number of mixes for different purposes; some of the 'preferred mixtures' are listed here. Asphalt mixtures are designated by BS numbers referring to the aggregate content related to the aggregate size:

- Road base, base course, regulating course – a regulating course is used to regulate the levels:
  Mixture 50/14; (preferred) 14 mm aggregate thickness 35–65 mm;
  Mixture 60/28; (preferred) 28 mm aggregate thickness 60–120 mm.
- Wearing course Design Type F:
  Mixture 30/14; (preferred) 14 mm aggregate thickness 40 mm;
  Mixture 40/14; (preferred) 14 mm aggregate thickness 50 mm.
- Wearing course Design Type C:
  Mixture 0/3; 2.36 mm aggregate thickness 25 mm;
  Mixture 30/14; 14 mm aggregate thickness 40 mm;
  Mixture 40/14; 14 mm aggregate thickness 50 mm;
  Mixture 55/10; 10 mm aggregate thickness 40 mm;
  Mixture 55/14; 14 mm aggregate thickness 45 mm.
  Although Type F and Type C look similar, the proportions of different sized aggregates vary between the two types. Mixtures 55/10 and 55/14 are not coated with chippings and are only used for secondary roads, estate roads, play areas and other lightly trafficked roadways where high-speed skidding is not likely.
- Design Type R:
  Mixture R30/14F; 14 mm aggregate thickness 40 mm;
  Mixture R40/14F; 14 mm aggregate thickness 50 mm;
  Mixture R30/14C; 14 mm aggregate thickness 40 mm;
  Mixture R40/14C; 14 mm aggregate thickness 50 mm.
  R Types are 'enriched mixtures' which are designed to prevent break-up caused by fatigue and for cold wet conditions, though they are more liable to deformation than Types F and C. Probably useful if the landscape designer should happen to be designing a deep-freeze store or a wet-fish loading bay, though there could genuinely be a need for R Type mixtures in wash-down bays for lorries. Traditional 'Recipe Type F' mixtures are now obsolete.

Laying hot rolled asphalt

The principles for the construction and laying of asphalt surfaced roadways are much the same as those for coated macadam roadways, but there are some variations which must be considered. In laying an asphalt surface, the close control of the 'paving train' (which comprises the asphalt laying machine, delivery vehicles, the chipping spreader, and an 8 tonne roller) is essential to keep the material at the proper temperature, properly compacted and properly levelled. This is why an apparently unreasonable length of road seems to be closed when asphalt laying is in progress, as hot asphalt is a sensitive substance and dislikes being trodden on until it has completely set. Hand laying of odd corners can be done alongside machine laying to ensure a good bond, and asphalt should be tamped hot by hand round manholes and other awkward corners (though the roller driver should take care not to flatten the hand workers).

Coated chippings are sometimes incorporated in the surface layer to prevent skidding; these are rolled in hot after the first layer of asphalt has been laid and compacted. Chippings for low skid resistance are laid as 60 per cent of total coverage, while chippings for high skid resistance are laid as 80 per cent of total coverage. No chippings should be laid for 150 mm adjoining the kerb so that run-off water can flow easily along the channel. Chippings laid too deep do not stop skids; chippings laid too high get dislodged.

Asphalt on new roadways

When laying asphalt on new roadways the following criteria must be applied:

- Variations in level from sub-base to asphalt surface should be +10 or −30 mm.
- Variations in level from road base to asphalt surface in trafficked roadways should be ±15mm.
- Variations in level from base course to asphalt surface in playgrounds or level roadways such as car parks should be ± 10mm.
- Straight crossfall on roadways and the camber from crown to channel (the middle of the road to the gutter) should be not less than 2 per cent (1:50) or more than 3 per cent (1:33), with a fall in the channel of 0.8 per cent (1:125). If these falls cannot be obtained, precast channels with their own falls should be used.
- No laying in frost or on ice or snow, or on a wet surface.
- Hand laid asphalt must be kept just as hot, but hand laying of odd corners can be done alongside machine laying.
- Where asphalt has to stick to walls or kerbs, these should be coated with hot bitumen before asphalting.

Asphalt on existing paving:

When laying asphalt on existing paving the following criteria must be applied:

- For new asphalt on concrete slab, clean and fill cracks and joints before laying.
- For new asphalt on sett or block paving, cut out weak spots and fill with concrete or asphalt base course mixture.
- Joints should be offset not less than 300 mm from the joints in the layers below.

2.3 MASTIC ASPHALT

It is composed of fine and coarse aggregate and 'asphaltic cement' which forms a cohesive impermeable material, solid or semi-solid, which can be hand laid without compaction. Mastic asphalt is used mostly for balconies, roof decks, roof gardens, multi-storey car parks, tanking and other situations where the full paving train used for hot rolled asphalt would find itself rather cramped.

Asphaltic cement is bitumen, lake asphalt, or asphaltite, or blends of these materials. Fine aggregate is either natural rock asphalt (limestone naturally impregnated with bitumen) or fine crushed limestone. Coarse aggregate is either crushed granite or limestone, or grit. Mastic asphalt should be laid to fall not less than 1:80, but it is better to design for 1:50 to allow for subsidence and construction errors. Typical construction would be:

- Lightly loaded areas such as play areas, drying grounds, ramps: overall thickness 25 mm
  base layer: one coat roofing grade asphalt;
  glass fibre separating membrane;
  top layer: one coat roofing grade asphalt with 5–10 per cent grit rolled in.
- Heavily loaded areas such as lorry loading and standing:
  base layer 20 mm thick: two coats roofing grade asphalt;
  glass fibre separating membrane;
  top layer 40 mm thick: paving grade asphalt.

To prevent the asphalt from being distorted by point wheel loads, metal lattices can be embedded in the top layer to stabilize the asphalt.

2.4 DENSE TAR SURFACING

Dense tar surfacing, or 'DTS', is a hot laid mixture of road tar, aggregate and filler which is used for the wearing course of roadways and paved areas where oil spillage is likely to be a problem. The relevant Standard is BS 5273. The aggregate and fillers are similar to those used in bitumen macadam mixtures. Depending on the traffic loading, DTS wearing course thicknesses can be:

40 mm thick with 10 mm aggregate;
40 mm thick with 14 mm aggregate;
30 mm thick with 10 mm aggregate;

The construction of the sub-base, road base, and wearing courses is the same as for coated macadam, and the same requirements for laying and detailing are applicable.

2.5 CONCRETE ROADWAYS

Complete concrete roads are very little used today, and hardly at all in landscape work. They have been replaced for urban paved areas and pedestrian routes by the 'interlocking block flexible pavement' which is discussed more fully under Concrete Blocks (see p. 52). Concrete used to be used for highways, but the noisy

Plate 4 *Tree roots cracking an asphalt footway. Such cracks can be easily repaired in monolithic paving by cutting out and filling with hot asphalt; cracked unit paving would have to be replaced.*

surface and poor performance compared with macadam roads have caused them to become obsolescent.

Like coated macadam roads, the design and construction of concrete roads is controlled by the *Department of Transport Specification for Highway Works*, Clauses 1000 to 1042. This is a very massive and complicated document intended for major road design which is unlikely to form part of the landscape contract, but nevertheless, the landscape designer should follow the DoT principles of construction; those most appropriate to landscape work have been included in this section.

Ordinary concrete is used for road construction, but concrete made with a blend of Portland cement and pfa (pulverized fuel ash) gives greater density, less permeability, and greater resistance to chemical attack. Concrete for the road base can be plain concrete, but the wearing surface is better made with air-entrained concrete which is not so strong but reduces permeability. Plasticizers to increase workability, and retarders to allow hot summer working are permitted; workability is a problem as stiff concrete is needed to hold reinforcement in place, while soft concrete is needed to texture the surface and work round odd corners.

Sub-bases or road bases can be made of 'wet lean concrete' which has less cement, and can be specified in four grades equivalent in strength to the Cement Bound Macadam grades CBM 1, CBM 2, CBM 3, and CBM 4 as described earlier. The grades of concrete for these layers and the wearing course are specified in the *Department of Transport Specification for Highway Works*, Clauses 1001 to 1006, and are summarized in Table 2.2. The maximum size of aggregate permitted for road work is 40 mm. The strength of the concrete for the wearing course should be not less than 48.2 N/mm², which allows for deviations in mixing and laying. Old names for concrete mixes are shown in brackets in Table 2.2.

A waterproof membrane must be laid on the sub-base to prevent water draining out of the concrete road base before it has set. A bit of slip between the sub-base and the road base is considered a good thing, but reinforced road bases should be laid on a bitumen emulsion spray instead to keep the upper layers in place. Freshly poured concrete must be 'cured', that is, protected from frost, heat and drying winds by covering it with plastic sheet, spraying it with water, or laying wet hessian sheeting topped with plastic sheet. Plastic can be sprayed on and peeled off later like a giant lolly wrapping.

A typical specification for a driveway for residential use would be concrete 100 mm thick for good sub-strate or concrete 150 mm thick for poor sub-strate laid on 100 mm hardcore using designated mix PAV1, with minimum cement content 300 kg/m³ and 5.5 per cent entrained air; 75 mm slump.

Table 2.2
Concrete road mixes

Roadway layer	Concrete mix to BS 5328 :Part 1
Sub-base or road base:	
wet lean concrete 1	ST 1 (C7.5, C7.5P)
wet lean concrete 2	ST 2 (C10, C10P)
wet lean concrete 3	ST 3 (C15, C15P)
wet lean concrete 4	ST 4 (C20, C20P)
Road base:	
continuously reinforced:	C40
Surface slab (wearing course):	
unreinforced	C40
jointed reinforced	C40
continuously reinforced	C40

Reinforced concrete

Reinforced concrete is used for roads where there is some danger of subsidence, or where roadways must pass over made ground. Reinforcement may be by means of steel bars laid in both directions, but light roads are usually reinforced with prefabricated steel mesh laid halfway through the thickness of the slab. The calculation of the reinforcement is the highway engineer's job, but typical reinforcement would be steel mesh to BS 4483, 200 × 200 mm square either 2.22 kg/m^2 or 3.02 kg/m^2.

Movement joints

Movement joints are contraction joints in the winter, and expansion joints in the summer – what the contractor calls them at the equinox is anybody's guess. Any change in thickness, material, or direction requires a movement joint. Correctly placed joints can help to control cracking, since cracks will develop along weak lines such as joints rather than in the middle of the slab.

Longitudinal joints should be at a maximum width of 4.2 m for unreinforced concrete, and a maximum width of 6.0 m for reinforced concrete with an offset between one layer and the next of 300 mm; they are formed in the wet concrete. Transverse joints in unreinforced slabs should be at spacings giving a longitudinal:transverse ratio no more than 2:1.

Transverse joints are filled with softboard and then, oddly enough, sawn after the concrete has just set, as pre-forming joints in the wet concrete may lead to distorted joints. The joints are filled after sawing with special sealants to BS 5212: Parts 1 and 2. Transverse joints should be offset not less than 1 m between one layer and the next. Try to keep manholes, gulley and access points generally away from the middle of concrete roads; if they must intrude, put them next to a movement joint.

Surfacing

The surface of the wearing course is textured to a depth of 1 mm to give a grip to tyres; less will permit skidding, more will be horribly noisy. Texturing is done by brushing the concrete just after it has set, and the judgement of the exact time and brush setting for this operation is a highly skilled affair.

Resurfacing

Old concrete which has worn smooth can be retextured by cutting transverse grooves 3 mm wide × 4 mm deep; this is supposed to cause less tyre noise than shallow narrow grooves.

3   UNIT PAVING

There are many types of unit paving, and many variants within each type. The principal types of unit paving described in this section are the following:

- standard and non-standard precast concrete flags;
- precast concrete blocks;
- natural stone slabs;
- granite setts and precast concrete setts;
- bricks and brick pavers;
- cobbles set in concrete;
- grass concrete paving;
- pedestrian deterrent paving.

Some traditional unit paving designs and their modern equivalents are shown in Figure 3.1.

Since the methods of laying the different types of unit paving are broadly similar, the construction of the sub-base is described in Section 1.1, and the methods of bedding and jointing are described on p. 42, with more specific information being given under each type of unit paving. The ancillary items such as kerbs, edgings, gullies and surface drains are described in a separate section, as most of these items are common to unit, monolithic and granular paving. Once upon a time end grain elm blocks were used to pave London streets (and horribly slippery they were in wet weather or frost) and although it is possible to get hardwood blocks for paving in sheltered areas, the conscientious landscape designer will be wary of endangering yet more forests. Hardwood plank walkways are feasible if the suppliers' claims for renewable timber can be believed, but they are not strictly paving, and they are discussed in Volume 3 of this series.

The components of a unit paving system are:

- *Sub-strate*: the natural or made-up ground brought to formation level.
- *Optional geotextile membrane*: prevents soil particles from intruding into the sub-base.
- *Sub-base*: granular material which provides a firm, well-drained and even foundation for the paving.

STEPCOTE HILL IN EXETER. *Pack-mule track in centre, pedestrian steps at each side.*

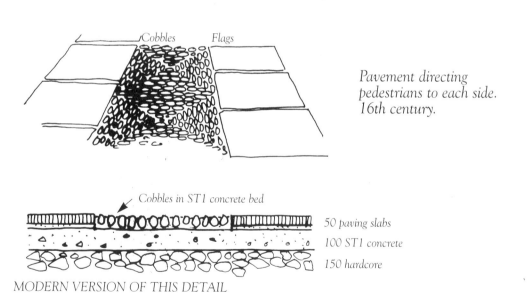

Steps   *Cobbles*   *Granite sett drain channel*   *Precast concrete kerb*

MODERN VERSION OF THIS DETAIL   *ST1 concrete bedding*   *150 DoT Type 1*

Cobbles   *Flags*

Pavement directing pedestrians to each side. 16th century.

Cobbles in ST1 concrete bed

50 paving slabs
100 ST1 concrete
150 hardcore

MODERN VERSION OF THIS DETAIL

Figure 3.1   Traditional pavements

40

- *Blinding*: fine layer of sand or ash spread on the sub-strate to fill large voids in the material.
- *Bedding*: sand, mortar, or other material which holds the paving firmly in position.
- *Paving units*: brick, concrete, grass concrete, or stone units as detailed by the landscape designer.
- *Jointing*: material used to fill the paving joints and to give the desired finish to the paving. Paving is either 'jointed' as the work proceeds, or 'pointed' afterwards.

The ability of the paving to prevent slipping is an important consideration for the landscape designer, and the manufacturer should always be asked to give the skid resistance of the product. Skid resistance is calculated in accordance with the Road Research Laboratory Road Note 27, and the resistance of the paving when wet or dry should lie between 40 and 74; a score of 20 to 39 is doubtful, while anything under 19 should be rejected as such paving is a hazard to vehicles and pedestrians. Paving with a skid resistance over 75 can be specified with confidence. This standard only applies to road surfaces, but work is being done to establish a standard applicable to all types of paving. In the meantime, the manufacturer of any paving material should be asked to give a written statement on the properties of the product.

Sub-base

The sub-base should be designed as described in Section 1.1, Bases for Roadways and Paving (see pages 5–15). Cement bound material sub-bases are more suitable for large areas of paving not subject to heavy loading, that is Class A as described at the beginning of Section 1.1. Expansion joints are normally not necessary. Approximate thicknesses for lightly loaded sub-bases are given in Section 1.1, but the material must be compacted in layers not exceeding 150 mm, though better results are obtained with 100 mm layers. Sub-base requirements for specific types of unit paving are described under the relevant heading. It may seem odd to refer to the supporting material for paving as a 'sub-base' rather than a 'base', but the term is derived from highway construction, where the sub-base is only one of several layers under the finished surface.

The sub-base for unit paving must be correctly specified for the type of paving and for the load which it must carry. Paving sub-bases where vehicle overrun occurs need to be designed almost as strongly as highway sub-bases, while domestic paving can be laid on a comparatively light sub-base. The options described in Section 1.1 are:

a solid concrete base;
a cement bound material sub-base;
a granular sub-base.

A concrete sub-base is required where the paving must be smooth, even, and stable under all foreseeable conditions. The areas where the landscape designer should consider a concrete sub-base include the entrances and paths around hospital and other health care buildings, pedestrian areas in shopping malls, old people's homes, schools, or indeed any other area where wheelchairs and disabled people are regular visitors. Of course, ideally all paving should remain in perfect condition throughout its life, but cost considerations may force the landscape designer to specify a paving system which is not totally proof against damage and settlement. The concrete should be C20P, that is a 1:2:4 cement:sand:aggregate mix with 20 mm aggregate, laid on well-rammed hardcore of broken brick, concrete or stone. Hardcore should be 100 mm thick as a minimum, and 150 mm is preferable, as it is not easy to get an even surface in a lesser thickness; if the sub-grade is very open in texture, it should be blinded with sand or ash before the concrete is laid, since sand is much cheaper than concrete. The concrete sub-base should be 75 mm minimum for areas restricted to pedestrians only (100 mm is better), and 150 mm for areas where cars are likely to use the paving. The falls in the paving which are designed to allow free draining of the surface must be established in this sub-base with a maximum variation to the designed falls of ± 10 mm. If the sub-grade is composed of much filled ground, or if there are many changes of level, light steel mesh reinforcement may be needed in the sub-base. For reinforced sub-bases, 100 mm is the minimum thickness, and the mesh must be placed halfway between the top and bottom of the concrete. Concrete 100 mm thick with reinforcing mesh 200 x 200 mm ref. A/142 to BS 4483, with head laps 300 mm and side laps 150 mm, will be adequate for light traffic, while concrete 150 mm thick with ref. A/193 mesh is usual for heavier loading.

Bedding and jointing generally

Bedding methods for specific types of unit paving are described under the relevant heading. Bedding is the operation of setting the paving units onto the sub-base so that they are level and stable. Where a concrete or lean-mix concrete sub-base is used, the units should be bedded in mortar, but where a granular or cement-bound sub-base is used, bedding in sand is preferable.

Mortar bedding and jointing

It is advisable to use a concrete sub-base for units bedded in mortar, as a granular sub-base is less rigid, though for domestic purposes bedding on well-compacted granular fill is acceptable. Mortar bedding is generally used for large flags, setts, cobbles, natural stone slabs, granite setts, and for bricks or brick pavers. For internal paving, such as covered shopping malls or internal courtyards, a 1:4 cement:sand mix should be used, while for external paving a 1:3 or 1:4 lime:sand mix should be used. Lime:sand mortar may be prepared on site, but it is preferable to specify ready-mixed material which is delivered to site as required, as lime is not an easy material to handle and mix successfully, and pockets of unmixed lime in the bedding can cause damage. It is a mistake to use either cement or lime mortar too strong, as cracking and shrinkage are more liable to occur. Beds are usually 25 mm thick; thicker beds result in the paving units 'squishing' into the bed and tipping, while too thin a bed does not allow any tolerance for slight inequalities in the sub-base. The jointing of paving units follows the technique used for bedding units; cement mortar joints for cement mortar beds, and lime:sand mortar for lime:sand beds. Joints may be formed as the units are laid, as in brickwork, but it is preferable to lay the units with open joints and to point them afterwards, as the work can be done more carefully and any damage made good before pointing. Units may be laid either with narrow joints 2 to 4 mm wide with dry fine sand brushed into the joint, or with wide joints 5 to 10 mm wide pointed with $1:4\frac{1}{2}$ cement:sand mortar finished 2 mm below the paving surface. Small paving units do not need special movement joints, as any movement can be absorbed by the many joints between units, but where there is a movement joint in the underlying layers this should be repeated in the paving.

Sand bedding and jointing

This bedding may be used for flags, concrete blocks, concrete setts, and for bricks and brick pavers where water penetration does not matter; it is generally used where units will have to be lifted and replaced for alterations and maintenance of piped services under the paving, as it is obviously easier to replace units bedded in sand than in mortar. It will always be a temptation to the landscape contractors to help themselves from the building contractor's sand pile, but the sands used for bricklaying and plastering are quite different from bedding sand and should not be used. Proper dry bedding sand can be supplied ready bagged and labelled to avoid accidental-on-purpose errors. In sand-bedded work it is essential to lay the edge restraint units first and to work up to them to prevent the units from being displaced during vibration.

The laying of small units is well described in BS 7263: Parts 1 and 2, which give details of materials and methods. Concrete blocks, sett paving, and brick paving may all be laid by bedding in sand and vibrating, which gives a very firm stable paving. The usual specification requires a sand bedding to Grades C or M of BS 882 which is laid on the sub-base and compacted to 25 mm; a further 10 mm of loose sand (grade F to BS 882) is then spread on this and the paving units are then laid closely together on this and vibrated with a special plate vibrator to bed them down and level them. After laying, fine dry sand is brushed into the joints and the paving is then vibrated again. Vibrated sand bedding is described in more detail in the Section on Concrete Blocks. This type of dry-laying is not suitable for paving with falls exceeding 1 in 10, as the units may creep.

3.1 FLAGS

The term 'flags' is usually used to mean precast concrete or reconstructed stone paving units, whereas the term 'slabs' usually implies sawn or naturally split stone. Flags may be either British Standard or non-standard. Sizes of British Standard flags are given in Table 3.1, and they must comply with requirements for strength, slip-resistance (there is no such thing as a perfectly 'non-slip' flag), wear, colour, size and shape. Flags for heavy public use, such as urban pavements, are hydraulically pressed to provide a hard-wearing surface, often treated with carborundum for extra slip-resistance; these are also resistant to de-icing salts. Some non-standard flags are similar in quality, but are cheaper and lighter types which are perfectly suitable for residential use, though they should not be used for vehicular or heavily used pedestrian areas unless they are specifically guaranteed by the manufacturer for this type of traffic. Almost any pattern of paving can be constructed using various sizes and layouts of flags, but patterns which mean a lot of cutting come expensive, and if the landscape designer wants a complex pattern it is preferable to use concrete blocks, setts, brick pavers or cobbles which have a much wider range of colours and textures. Flags are most commonly laid with a simple broken bond of single size units staggered; the bond may be achieved by using mixed sizes, though where underground services pass below the paving it is sensible to lay a straight jointed section (sometimes in a different colour) to make lifting and replacing the flags easier. Typical layouts are shown in Figure 3.2.

British Standard flags

Standard flags are manufactured to BS 7263: Part 1. The Standard includes requirements for transverse strength and moisture absorption, and the sizes shown in Table 3.1 and Figure 3.3 are available, specified either by letter reference or size and thickness.

The 'small unit' flags E, F and G are slightly chamfered at the edges. These used to be recommended for vehicle overrun, but there is now some evidence that a heavy vehicle with a large point load on a wheel can 'punch' the very small flags through into the base layer, leaving a dangerous tripping edge for pedestrians, and the 400 x 400 mm or 450 x 450 mm flag is now recommended. Where HGVs are expected either concrete paving blocks, granite setts or monolithic paving specifically designed to carry heavy loads are preferable. The landscape designer will have to decide which advice to follow, but the best precaution against damaged paving is to ensure that the sub-base is designed to take the expected loading, and that it is properly laid and compacted. For some reason, unevenness in large flags is more perceptible than in small ones, so that people are less likely to trip over raised edges.

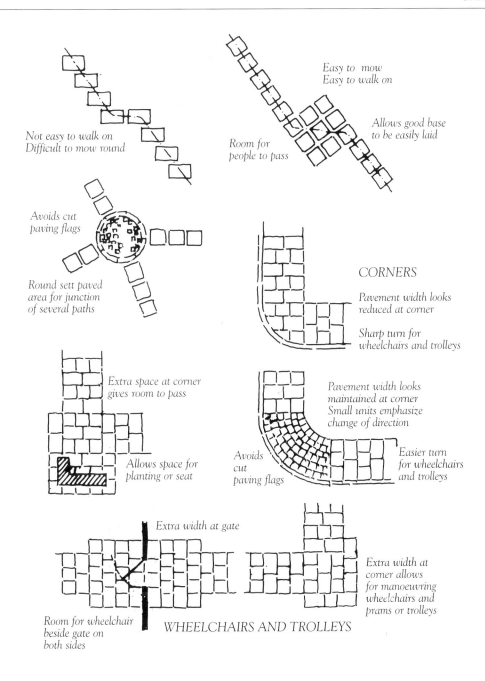

Not easy to walk on
Difficult to mow round

Easy to mow
Easy to walk on

Allows good base
to be easily laid

Room for
people to pass

Avoids cut
paving flags

Round sett paved
area for junction
of several paths

CORNERS

Pavement width looks
reduced at corner

Sharp turn for
wheelchairs and trolleys

Extra space at corner
gives room to pass

Pavement width looks
maintained at corner
Small units emphasize
change of direction

Allows space for
planting or seat

Avoids
cut
paving flags

Easier turn
for wheelchairs
and trolleys

Extra width at gate

Extra width at
corner allows
for manoeuvring
wheelchairs and
prams or trolleys

Room for wheelchair
beside gate on
both sides

WHEELCHAIRS AND TROLLEYS

Figure 3.2 Paving layouts

	Table 3.1	British Standard flags	
	Reference	Nominal size (mm)	Thickness (mm)
Pedestrian areas and occasional cars, residential driveways			
	A	600 × 450	50 and 63
	B	600 × 600	50 and 63
	C	600 × 750	50 and 63
	D	600 × 900	50 and 63
	E	450 × 450	50 and 70 chamfered top edges
	F	400 × 400	50 and 65 chamfered top edges
	G	300 × 300	50 and 60 chamfered top edges
Light traffic, service access, fire paths			
	A	600 × 450	63
	B	600 × 600	63
	E	450 × 450	70
	F	400 × 400	65
	G	300 × 300	60
Heavy vehicle overrun			
	E	450 × 450	70
	F	400 × 400	65
	G	300 × 300	60

Note: Nominal size means that there is a working clearance so that the laid flags meet the dimensions given.

Non-standard flags

Non-standard flags are made in a very wide range of colours, sizes and textures, and provide the landscape designer with the opportunity to design highly ornamental paving. Precast concrete flags can be had with textured surfaces which have been cast from a mould taken from natural stone slabs, and faced with stone dust from the quarry, so that the surface resembles the natural stone very closely, although the artificial product is never as beautiful as the real stone. These textured flags are not suitable for heavily used paving, as when the textured face wears off the flags look no better than the standard plain surface flag. Where flags are laid as a decorative paving rather than as a trafficked paving, aggregate faced flags can be used. These are cast with a surface of natural aggregate such as grey, brown, or golden gravel; chippings of stone such as creamy-white, golden pink, or

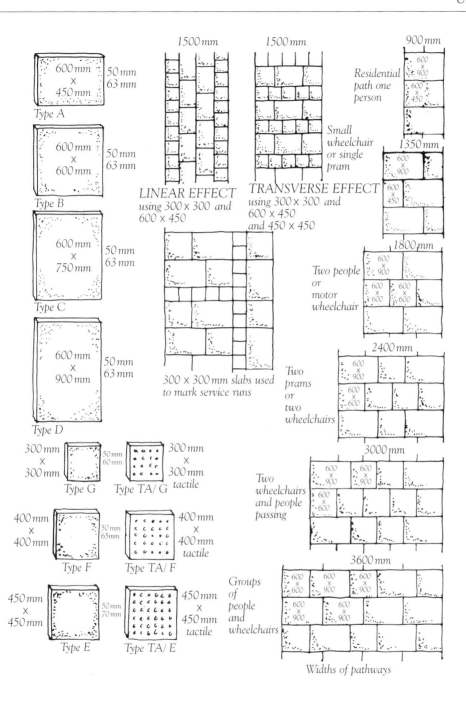

Type A 600 mm × 450 mm — 50 mm / 63 mm

Type B 600 mm × 600 mm — 50 mm / 63 mm

Type C 600 mm × 750 mm — 50 mm / 63 mm

Type D 600 mm × 900 mm — 50 mm / 63 mm

Type G 300 mm × 300 mm — 50 mm / 60 mm

Type TA/ G 300 mm × 300 mm tactile

Type F 400 mm × 400 mm — 50 mm / 65 mm

Type TA/ F 400 mm × 400 mm tactile

Type E 450 mm × 450 mm — 50 mm / 70 mm

Type TA/ E 450 mm × 450 mm tactile

1500 mm 1500 mm

LINEAR EFFECT
using 300 × 300 and
600 × 450

TRANSVERSE EFFECT
using 300 × 300 and
600 × 450
and 450 × 450

300 × 300 mm slabs used
to mark service runs

900 mm — Residential path one person — 600 × 900, 600 × 450

Small wheelchair or single pram

1350 mm — 600 × 900, 600 × 450

1800 mm — Two people or motor wheelchair — 600 × 900, 600 × 600

2400 mm — Two prams or two wheelchairs — 600 × 900, 600 × 600

3000 mm — Two wheelchairs and people passing — 600 × 900, 600 × 600

3600 mm — Groups of people and wheelchairs — 600 × 600, 600 × 900, 600 × 900

Widths of pathways

Figure 3.3   British Standard paving flags

brown Derbyshire Spar; grey or pink granite; white German quartz, and natural grey or calcined white crushed stone. These materials are very attractive and can be used to create colourful framing to ornamental planting, but they are unsuitable for prams and wheelchairs, as well as being spoilt by mud and chewing gum trodden into them.

Tactile flags

There are also specially textured concrete 'tactile' flags used to guide blind people to crossings and other key points which are also covered by the British Standard; they are available in three sizes with the references TA/E 450 x 450 mm, TA/F 400

Plate 5 *Precast fine finish concrete paving units by Blanc de Bierges used to form a shallow step. (Photograph by courtesy of Blanc de Bierges.)*

Plate 6 *Textured precast concrete flags with wide contrasting joints. This elegant texturing is better suited to domestic work than to public areas. (Photograph by courtesy of Blanc de Bierges.)*

x 400 mm, and TA/G 300 x 300 mm. These are usually installed in connection with 'cross now' audible signals and are mandatory where the pedestrian route crosses a carriageway. Also available are rubber tactile tiles which can be fixed to new or existing concrete surfaces; these tiles are 400 x 400 mm, and are made in three types to Department of Transport standards:

- wide spaced raised dots for pedestrian crossings to roads (red for controlled crossings, buff for uncontrolled crossings – useful for blind people!);
- close spaced raised dots for platform edges (black);
- ribs for directional guidance through wide open pedestrian areas; the ribs follow the direction of travel.

49

Sub-bases for flags

The design of sub-bases is described in greater detail in Section 1.1. Flags may be laid on a concrete sub-base or a granular sub-base. Since flags are not recommended for roadways or other areas which have to take vehicles, a lighter sub-base than that used for roadways is acceptable. Concrete sub-bases should be ST 5 (C25P) concrete with 20 mm aggregate at least 100 mm thick, laid on at least 100 m of well-rammed hardcore. Granular sub-bases are constructed as described in Section 1.1. All falls for drainage should be constructed in the sub-strate and followed in the sub-base, as attempts to make up drainage falls in the bedding and finish will cause uneven settlement and irregularities in the finished surface.

Bedding flags

The bedding and jointing of paving is described in greater detail on pages 42–43, and more detailed recommendations are given in BS 7263: Part 2. Flags laid on a suitable sub-base may be laid with either:

- five spot mortar (not recommended except for very cheap work);
- semi-dry mortar;
- wet mortar;
- sand bedding.

Five spot mortar bedding is used only for the lightest of paved areas, and is not really suitable for landscape contracts. The various methods of bedding are shown in Figure 3.4.

Semi-dry mortar bedding allows easier positioning of flags, but where vehicles are expected, wet mortar bedding gives the firmest support to the flags. The mortar bed should be screeded to give an even layer not less than 25 mm thick at any point, and the flags should be laid so that there is no more than 3 mm difference of level between adjoining flags, and no more than 6 mm variation from the designed levels. The mortar should be a lime:sand mix of 1:3 or 4; but as discussed elsewhere lime mortars are more difficult to mix well on site than cement mortars and are best supplied ready-mixed by specialist suppliers. If the flags are to be laid with narrow 2–3 mm joints they should be pointed with dry concreting sand (grade F to BS 882) brushed well into the joints. However, should the landscape designer prefer wide joints of 5–10 mm, they should be pointed with 1:3 or 4 cement:sand mortar carefully packed into the whole depth of the joint and left 2 mm or so below the finished surface; any mortar smears must be cleaned off immediately with plenty of clean water. Wide joints offer the landscape designer the chance to use a contrasting coloured mortar to enhance the pattern of the paving; it is perfectly possible to use wide joints one way and narrow joints the other way to emphasize a particular direction, though this arrangement will not be at all popular with the paviour laying the flags. Coloured mortar comes in a very wide range of colours and it is better to specify ready-mixed mortar from a specialist supplier, as colours mixed

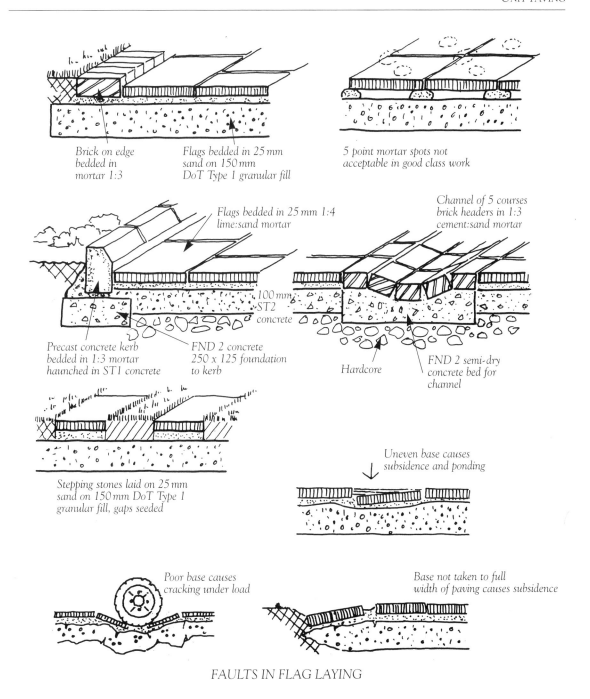

Brick on edge
bedded in
mortar 1:3

Flags bedded in 25 mm
sand on 150 mm
DoT Type 1 granular fill

5 point mortar spots not
acceptable in good class work

Flags bedded in 25 mm 1:4
lime:sand mortar

Channel of 5 courses
brick headers in 1:3
cement:sand mortar

100 mm
ST2
concrete

Precast concrete kerb
bedded in 1:3 mortar
haunched in ST1 concrete

FND 2 concrete
250 x 125 foundation
to kerb

Hardcore

FND 2 semi-dry
concrete bed for
channel

Stepping stones laid on 25 mm
sand on 150 mm DoT Type 1
granular fill, gaps seeded

Uneven base causes
subsidence and ponding

Poor base causes
cracking under load

Base not taken to full
width of paving causes subsidence

FAULTS IN FLAG LAYING

Figure 3.4   Bedding and laying flags

51

into mortar on site may result in piebald or streaky joints not intended by the landscape designer.

Sand-bedded flags are laid in 25 mm sand laid on the sub-base and the joints filled with dry sand. The most rigorous specification for flag paving calls for special types of sand (though it is unlikely that the average landscape designer will be able to identify a particular sand type on site) which allow for proper stabilization of the flags. Bedding sand should be specified as medium to coarse concreting sand, grade C or M to BS 882, and the jointing sand should be grade F. Where 'small unit paving' is being used, it should be bedded on sand and vibrated in the same way as for concrete block paving.

3.2 CONCRETE BLOCKS

Precast concrete blocks laid in plain bonds are the usual material for regular or occasional vehicular traffic; but interlocked blocks are more satisfactory for severely stressed paved areas such as bus stations and goods yards. When correctly laid such blocks can withstand the sideways pressure of turning wheels better than plain flags or brick pavers – nothing stresses paving more than heavy vehicles twisting round in a tight space. For these areas two types of block laying are usually specified:

- *Herring-bone*: plain blocks laid in alternate V-shaped patterns. Ideally the V of the pattern points in the direction of vehicle travel so that intemperate braking locks the blocks more firmly in place.
- *Shaped interlocking*: wiggly blocks which lock into each other.

Areas such as bus station forecourts are worst affected, since heavy buses pulling in and out on full lock and wheel-tracking over the same small patch of paving every day cause severe stress. Blocks for these areas should be not less than 100 mm thick. Where pedestrians are the only traffic using the paving, plain blocks may be laid in:

- 'stack bond': straight joints in both directions;
- 'half-bond': straight joints one way, staggered joints the other way;
- 'quarter-bond' as half-bond but smaller stagger;
- 'basket-weave' two blocks laid one way, then two laid the other way.

The British Standard for concrete blocks is BS 6717: Part 1, which governs the size, strength and materials of the blocks. There are two types of block:

- Type R blocks are rectangular 200 x 100 mm;
- Type S blocks can be any shape fitting into a 295 mm square.

Plate 7 *Laying precast concrete block paving 1. Edge restraint bedded in concrete before laying the blocks.*

Both types must be not less than 60 mm thick, and standard thicknesses are 60, 65, 80 and 100 mm.

Specially shaped blocks are made for infill edging to patterns, kerbs, drainage channels, circular work and for filling man-hole covers to match the paving. Excellent guidance on the detailed design of heavily loaded paved areas and public roads may be obtained from the Concrete Block Paving Association. This covers all aspects of laying concrete blocks.

Block paving may be quite plain, with uniform coloured blocks laid in a stack or bonded pattern, or it may be dazzling with swirling patterns and strongly contrasting coloured blocks in stripes, squares, zig-zags, or circles.

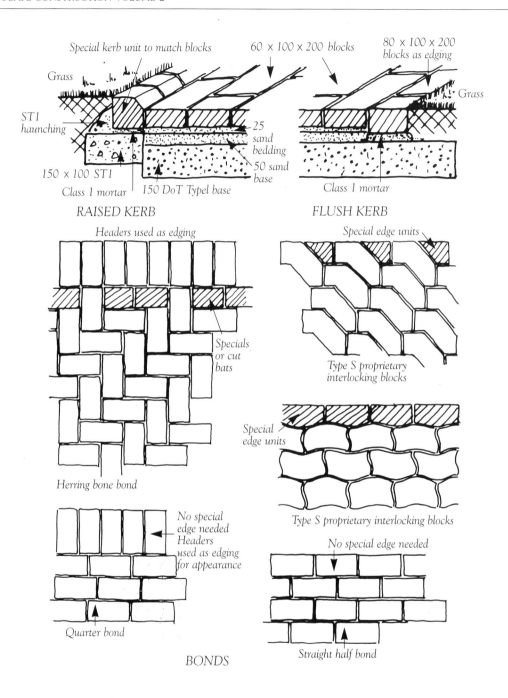

Special kerb unit to match blocks

60 × 100 × 200 blocks

80 × 100 × 200 blocks as edging

Grass

Grass

ST1 haunching

25 sand bedding

50 sand base

150 × 100 ST1

Class 1 mortar

150 DoT Type1 base

Class 1 mortar

RAISED KERB

FLUSH KERB

Headers used as edging

Special edge units

Specials or cut bats

Type S proprietary interlocking blocks

Herring bone bond

Special edge units

Type S proprietary interlocking blocks

No special edge needed Headers used as edging for appearance

No special edge needed

Quarter bond

Straight half bond

BONDS

Figure 3.5   Interlocking block paving

54

Plate 8 *Laying precast concrete block paving 2. Levelling the sand bedding for precast concrete block paving.*

Variations in colour and pattern are often used to define pedestrian/vehicle areas, to demarcate parking bays, or to form logos, crests or direction signs in the paving. They are not quite so obvious as vertical signs as they disappear under snow, mud or parked cars, but they are pretty well vandal-proof and permanent. This can be a snag when the business is taken over by another firm who do not wish to advertise their predecessor's products. It is not advisable to place logos or signs over underground service runs, as replacing the blocks later with a different colour might lead to misunderstandings. Most patterns can be made with standard blocks, but 'specials' for edges of patterns and signs can be made to order, though

Plate 9 *Laying precast concrete block paving 3. Vibrating the sand bedding.*

these are obviously more expensive. The laying of interlocking concrete blocks and some of the more common patterns are shown in Figure 3.5.

Sub-bases for concrete blocks

In the foreword to British Standard 7533, it is stated that, 'Research has indicated that block paving behaves in a similar manner to conventional flexible pavement construction materials'. This suggests that the landscape designer will find that the basic construction (at least for lightly trafficked roads and paving) will have similar sub-bases to that for macadam roadways.

Concrete blocks are laid on a granular sub-base for which the CBR (California Bearing Ratio) must be calculated as described in the Section 1.1, Bases for Roadways and Paving. Department of Transport Type 1 material only should be used for block paving, as Type 2 materials may be susceptible to moisture movement on damp sites, and where there is a considerable risk of frost (possibly paving to ski resorts in Scotland) the sub-base thickness should be at least 350 mm. Block paving should be laid to a fall of not less than 1.25 per cent (1:80) lengthways and 2.5 per cent (1:40) crossways, and these falls must be set out in the sub-base.

Plate 10 *Laying precast concrete block paving 4. Laying the blocks in herring bone pattern. Note that accurate sand levelling ensures that the blocks are laid level.*

Bedding concrete blocks

Although blocks may be bedded in mortar in the same way as flags, they are most often bedded in sand. Sand for bedding and jointing should be specified to comply with Table 2 of BS 6717: Part 3, which gives a complex mix of sand particle sizes which add up to a suitable sand. The best practice is to lay 50 mm of loose sand screeded accurately to the correct paving profile (allowing for the falls and crossfalls required for good drainage), then compact it with a vibrating plate compactor. On top of this compacted layer, lay 15 mm of loose sand screeded to the same profile for bedding the blocks. The bedding sand must not be compacted too hard, or the blocks will not settle. The blocks should be laid with open joints 2 mm to 5 mm wide, and it is essential that the edge restraint should be in position before the blocks are laid in order to prevent the blocks creeping when they are vibrated. After laying the blocks are vibrated again to bring them to the finished level and to settle them into their bed; at this stage some of the bedding sand will rise up into the joints and lock the blocks in place. Finally the joints are filled with dry sand well brushed in, and given a last pass of the vibrator to settle the sand into the joints; surplus sand is then brushed off. Both the blocks and the sand must be quite

Plate 11 *Laying precast concrete block paving 5. Blocks cut to fit curved edge. As this edging is only a shallow curve, special radial blocks are not necessary.*

dry when the joints are filled, as otherwise the sand will not penetrate the full depth of the joint. It is sensible to leave this surplus sand on the surface until the end of the contract, as it will absorb any stains and protect the surface from damage. Some manufacturers of concrete blocks supply special limestone grit which tends to consolidate, while another method of firming the joints is to use special bonding liquid which helps to prevent erosion. Block manufacturers may have slightly different recommendations for laying their own product.

When laying concrete blocks, the edge restraint, whether special unit, kerb, edging or wall, should be constructed before the paving is laid. First the whole blocks are laid to the desired pattern, then special shaped blocks or cut blocks are used for edge filling. Cut blocks must be cut with a proper block-cutter, as chopping them up with a hammer and bolster is likely to leave the block with internal shattering which (of course) only appears after the paving is in use.

Plate 12 *Laying precast concrete block paving 6. Blocks cut to fit manhole cover. Note the use of half blocks outside the cover to maintain the bonding.*

3.3 NATURAL STONE SLABS

These are perhaps the most expensive of paving materials, with the possible exception of special terracotta tiles. Stone slabs are split mechanically or by hand, or sawn, according to the natural planes of the rock. A sawn finish will be very smooth, while a riven finish will have slight variations in the plane of its surface, depending on the way in which the stone splits. The riven stone is the most attractive to look at since each slab will vary from its neighbours, but the landscape designer must beware of slabs with too large a variation in the surface, as depressions in the stone may hold water with consequent freezing and spalling. There is no British Standard for natural stone paving, so the landscape designer must rely on the quarry's advice on the most suitable types and sizes of stone for the contract. Natural split stone, and indeed sawn stone as well, should always be laid to a good fall in both directions. Old-time stone masons will say that the stone should be seasoned like timber to dry out the 'quarry sap' which is the natural moisture present in the stone, and this seems to be a sensible idea.

It is unlikely that the landscape designer will be offered flat stone slabs sawn against the bed, but it is worth checking that the slabs have been cut so that they lie (as they did in the quarry) with the natural bed planes of the stone lying horizontally. This is easy to check with large flat slabs, but not so easy with square section kerbs and small sett sized stones. 'Sur-bedding', with the natural planes vertical, will result in rapid water penetration and consequent spalling.

There are some old paths in historic towns where steep slopes have been laid with small paving slabs set sur-bedded; this creates a serrated surface which gives a good grip to men and mules carrying loads up or down hill, and the constant slight flaking away of the bed edges keeps the surface in rough condition. Horse or foot traffic, especially with unshod beasts, does not damage this surface quickly enough to matter. Such a technique might be useful for steep footpaths where the traffic is limited to soft-soled boots and animals. Some traditional paving layouts are shown in Figure 3.6.

The most frequently available types of natural stone in the UK are the following:

- York stone: yellowish-brown to blue-grey with good slip resistance and a slight sparkle. Reclaimed York stone from old city pavements is readily available, and the worn surfaces are smoother than new stone. Very badly worn slabs should be turned over and the underside dressed to a level plane, though the minimum thickness should not be less than 40 mm; this is for light pedestrian only paving.
- Portland Whitbed: creamy-white shell-flecked, available in squared flags up to 800 × 800 × 75 mm.
- Donegal Quartzite: green-olive-gold, available in sizes 150 to 400 mm wide and random lengths 20 to 35 mm thick.
- Liscannor Flagstone: yellowish-blue-grey, textured surface very resistant to atmospheric and chemical attack, available 150 to 600 mm wide random lengths, 19 to 55 mm thick.
- Slate slabs are readily available, but they soon lose their texture under wear, and they can be slippery in wet weather, so that their lovely blue-green-bronze tints are best displayed in sheltered areas or for purely ornamental paving.
- Marble paving is better used indoors in the UK climate, though the rather rough marble stone from the Mediterranean can be used in sheltered places.
- There are many local stones such as ironstone, Kentish Rag, blue rag, and local sandstones and limestones which have traditionally been used for paving, but most of these quarries are closed for commercial supplies, and the landscape designer would be lucky to find a source today. Even so, it is always worth asking if good local stone is available, especially in traditional stone-working districts. Sometimes second-hand stone from old farms or canal works can be found in small quantities.

Fine grained stone such as York stone can be obtained in several different finishes:

- Diamond sawn, which gives a fine non-directional finish.
- Shot sawn, which gives slight ridging in the direction of cut.
- Riven, which is the natural stone split and left; this can be rather uneven to walk on.
- Flame textured, which gives a crystalline very slip-resistant finish, though the surface does not look quite like the natural stone.
- Fine rubbed, which is really more suitable for indoor work.

Most stone is supplied to standard widths ranging from 450 to 750 mm and in random lengths up to 900 or 1200 mm according to the type of stone. As nearly all natural stone is cut to order, the landscape designer can specify any size of slab within the natural strength of the rock, remembering that the bigger the slab the thicker and more expensive it will be. Thicknesses usually supplied are 40 mm for residential use, 50 mm for public pedestrian use, 65 mm for car parking, and 75 mm for heavy vehicle overrun: natural stone is both unsuitable and too expensive for use on trafficked roads.

There is a technique known as 'flame texturing' which is carried out by some stone suppliers. This consists of treating the stone with a very high temperature fire so that the surface becomes crystallized, much as it would do in natural geological conditions, producing an attractive sparkling finish which has the merit of being very slip-resistant. Although this adds to the cost of the stone, it may be well worth while where good foothold and a crisp appearance are valuable. Stone which can be treated in this way include York stone, limestone, slate and quartzite.

Irregular paving

Variants on formal regular stone paving are 'crazy paving' (more politely called 'random paving') and stepping stones.

Random paving has been decried as a cheap alternative to 'proper' stone paving. Although most random paving seen in suburban gardens is made of broken concrete flags supplied by the local authority, well laid paving constructed of split and broken slabs from naturally laminated and fractured stone such as slate or some types of limestone can be most attractive. This paving should be laid and bedded as for formal paving, but as the joints are more irregular and wider than the standard 3 or 6 mm joints a great deal of care is needed to achieve a good appearance. Owing to the random nature of the material it is impossible to work out a pattern for this paving on the drawing board, thus the laying and jointing is a very skilled job and only experienced paviours should be employed for the work. Where joints are more than 15–20 mm wide it is usual to use 'galleting' which is a filling made either of small pieces of the same stone or a contrasting stone (or pebbles) set into the joints flush with the paving. The edging to random paving is

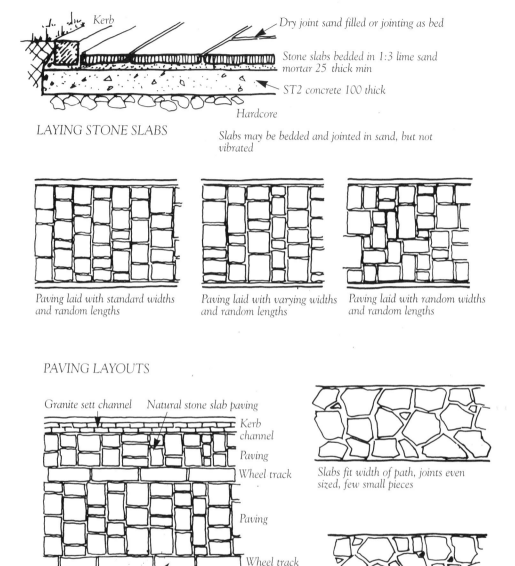

LAYING STONE SLABS

Kerb

Dry joint sand filled or jointing as bed

Stone slabs bedded in 1:3 lime sand mortar 25 thick min

ST2 concrete 100 thick

Hardcore

Slabs may be bedded and jointed in sand, but not vibrated

Paving laid with standard widths and random lengths

Paving laid with varying widths and random lengths

Paving laid with random widths and random lengths

PAVING LAYOUTS

Granite sett channel   Natural stone slab paving

Kerb channel

Paving

Wheel track

Paving

Wheel track

Paving

Channel kerb

Re-conditioned granite kerbs laid flat

STONE PAVED CARRIAGE WAY WITH GRANITE WHEEL TRACKS FOR VEHICLES

Slabs fit width of path, joints even sized, few small pieces

Slabs wrong size for width of path, too many small pieces, uneven joints

RANDOM PAVING

Figure 3.6   Natural stone paving

Plate 13   *Natural stone flags forming a path through a cobbled yard. Note how the emphasis on direction is made by laying the slabs either across or along the line of travel.*

the most difficult part of the design, and the paved area ought to be designed to a module of the average sized piece of stone in order to reduce the amount of cutting needed, as an artificially cut edge spoils the natural appearance of the paving. There is little point in using this paving for straight paths, and it is most suitable for serpentine or irregular paths or circular work.

Stepping stones can be made of ordinary or non-standard precast concrete flags, but as each stone is conspicuous in its isolation, natural stone is a more pleasant material to use. It is difficult to make a satisfactory bedding for a single stone, and there is an advantage in forming a continuous bedding layer the full length of the paving and filling the gaps between the stepping stones with open grid grass concrete blocks. The finished path will then look like grass and stones, but will have a good support capable of taking wheelbarrows or maintenance machinery without subsidence. The spacing and size of stepping stone is very important if a smooth pace for the pedestrian is to be attained. A normal easy walking pace for an adult is about 625 mm, and the stone spacing should be a module of this dimension; the stones may be any size as long as the minimum dimension is

300 mm to take the whole foot. While this spacing may give the path a rather regular look, it will be comfortable to walk on, and a random effect can be obtained by varying the width and shape of the stones. Stepping stones should not be used where elderly or disabled people must use them, and in this case it is sensible to provide an alternative route of continuous paving.

Sub-bases and bedding for natural stone slabs

The calculations for sub-bases for natural stone paving are the same as those for precast concrete flags, and should be carried out as described in Section 1.1, Bases for Roadways and Paving. A weak concrete sub-base laid on a capping layer of 150 mm well-rammed hardcore is normally satisfactory for lightly loaded areas. Hard limestones and dense slate are best bedded in 1:3 or 4 cement: sand, but softer stones should be bedded in the more accommodating 1:3 or 4 lime:sand mortar. A 25 mm bed is minimal, and as natural stone varies somewhat in thickness, the bedding will require more mortar to maintain the minimum thickness than man-made flags. Wide joints may occur if the slabs are not perfectly true (and also in random paving), which may be pointed with a lime:sand mortar, but if the joints are all less than 3 mm, they may be sand-filled. Stone slabs can be bedded in sharp concreteing sand with a minimum thickness of 25 mm, but they are not normally vibrated. The method of bedding natural stone slabs is shown in Figure 3.6.

3.4 SETTS

Setts, whether natural granite or precast concrete, are best used in areas where a very small scale paving pattern is required, or where the design involves complicated turns in the pathway. Setts are the ideal paving for creating circular patterns, as their small size means that they do not have to be cut to angles, any variation being taken up in the joints. The layout of circular sett features is illustrated in Figure 3.7. Historically, granite setts were used extensively in Scotland for roads in towns, where they are still standing up to modern traffic, though they are both noisy and bone-shaking, especially for cyclists. Granite setts were also used in the industrial towns in the docks, goods yards, and factory yards where they were almost the only surface capable of standing up to the heavy usage.

Granite setts

The sizes and quality of granite setts is covered by BS 435. Standard sizes are:

100 x 100 x 100 mm	100 x 100 x 150 to 250 mm
75 x 125 x 150 to 250 mm	100 x 125 x 150 to 250 mm
75 x 150 x 150 to 250 mm	100 x 150 x 150 to 250 mm

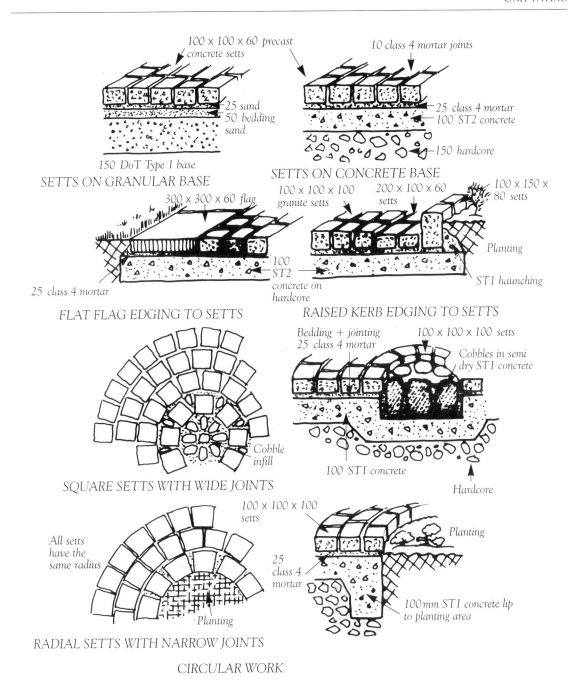

100 × 100 × 60 precast concrete setts

10 class 4 mortar joints

25 sand
50 bedding sand

25 class 4 mortar
100 ST2 concrete

150 hardcore

150 DoT Type 1 base

SETTS ON GRANULAR BASE

SETTS ON CONCRETE BASE

300 × 300 × 60 flag

100 × 100 × 100 granite setts

200 × 100 × 60 setts

100 × 150 × 80 setts

Planting

100 ST2 concrete on hardcore

25 class 4 mortar

ST1 haunching

FLAT FLAG EDGING TO SETTS

RAISED KERB EDGING TO SETTS

Bedding + jointing 25 class 4 mortar

100 × 100 × 100 setts

Cobbles in semi dry ST1 concrete

Cobble infill

SQUARE SETTS WITH WIDE JOINTS

100 ST1 concrete

Hardcore

All setts have the same radius

100 × 100 × 100 setts

25 class 4 mortar

Planting

100 mm ST1 concrete lip to planting area

Planting

RADIAL SETTS WITH NARROW JOINTS

CIRCULAR WORK

Figure 3.7   Setts

65

Setts may not vary more than 10 mm from these sizes. Other sizes are available to order.

New granite setts are now being quarried, and are more likely to be specified, since the supply of reclaimed setts from old city streets is drying up.

- New Portuguese setts are black-grey, 100 x 100 x 100 mm, 100 x 100 x 200 mm, 100 x 150 x 200 mm, 100 x 50 x 100 mm; specials can be supplied.
- Split reclaimed Scottish granite setts are given a new face by splitting, grey or pink with a fine sparkle, available 100 x 100 mm x random thicknesses.
- New (and more expensive) Scottish granite setts, grey or pink sparkling, to British Standard sizes or specials to order. The extreme cost of handhewn special granite setts will certainly deter all but the very rich client from using them in large areas.

Concrete setts

These are manufactured as a cheaper substitute for the much more expensive natural granite setts. Special shapes for small radius circles can be made which look better than cut setts. Concrete setts can be coloured and textured to give a pleasant appearance, but they lack the sparkle and subtle variations of the natural stone, although most manufacturers make their setts with a slightly rough surface resembling the natural hewn surface of granite. Like all ornamental concrete paving, they are liable to staining by oil and chemicals, and it is not sensible to use them in vehicular areas, where the cheaper and stronger concrete block is more suitable. The sizes of concrete setts vary between manufacturers, but a typical size range would be:

140 x 140 x 80 mm
210 x 140 x 80 mm
115 x 115 x 60 mm
 70 x 70 x 70 mm

Sub-bases and bedding

The design of sub-bases is described in Section 1.1, Bases for Roadways and Paving, and the bedding and jointing of paving is described in Bedding and Jointing Generally (pages 42–43). Setts which must carry heavy traffic should be laid on a reinforced concrete sub-base and bedded in 1:3 cement:sand mortar at least 25 mm thick, and should be laid closely butted with fine sand-filled joints. For pedestrian traffic and cars a granular sub-base will be satisfactory with the setts bedded in sand. Sand for bedding and jointing should comply with Table 2 of BS 6717: Part 3. The setts are laid on 50 mm of loose sand screeded accurately to the correct paving profile and compacted with a vibrating plate compactor. The bedding sand must not be compacted too hard, or the units will not settle. The paving joints are filled with dry sand and the whole surface compacted; for

Plate 14 *Circular paving feature in new grey and pink granite setts with slate circle. Architect: Eachus Huckson. Materials supplied by Civil Engineering Developments, Specialists in Natural Stone. (Photograph by courtesy of Civil Engineering Developments Ltd.)*

heavy granite a paviour's maul may be needed rather than a plate vibrator.

Concrete setts can also be laid in lime:sand mortar on a concrete sub-base, but they are usually laid on a granular sub-base, bedded on 50 mm compacted sand, vibrated, and the joints filled with sand in the same way as concrete block paving. Both methods of bedding are illustrated in Figure 3.7.

3.5 BRICKS AND BRICK PAVERS

Clay brick paving has been replaced to a great extent by concrete paving, partly because concrete paving is cheaper, and partly because concrete can be made in lighter colours than most clay bricks. Clay brick paving has natural variations in colour and texture which create more interesting and subtle paving.

Plate 15 *Precast concrete setts by Blanc de Bierges used to form interlocking circular feature in a Golden Award garden at Chelsea Flower Show by Merrist Wood College. (Photograph by courtesy of Blanc de Bierges.)*

Four types of brick can be used for paving:

- hard frost-resistant and sulphate resistant clay bricks;
- special clay brick 'pavers';
- clay engineering bricks;
- some classes of calcium silicate bricks.

Ordinary building bricks are neither hard enough nor frost resistant enough.

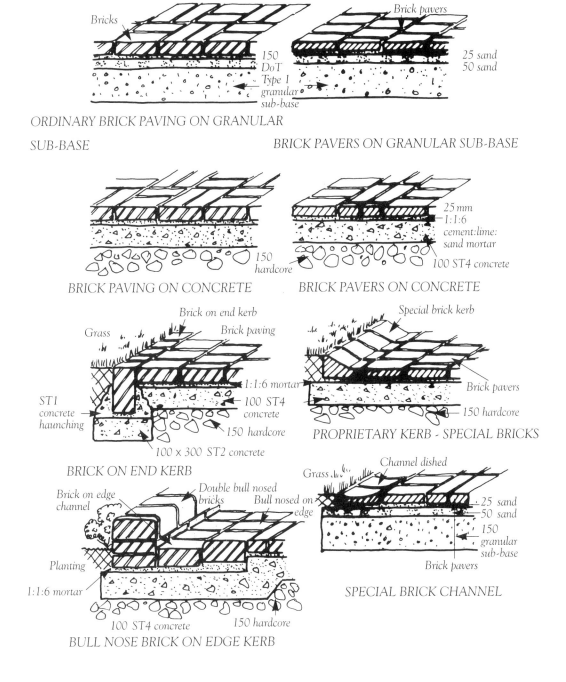

ORDINARY BRICK PAVING ON GRANULAR SUB-BASE

BRICK PAVERS ON GRANULAR SUB-BASE

BRICK PAVING ON CONCRETE

BRICK PAVERS ON CONCRETE

BRICK ON END KERB

PROPRIETARY KERB - SPECIAL BRICKS

BULL NOSE BRICK ON EDGE KERB

SPECIAL BRICK CHANNEL

Figure 3.8   Brick paving and pavers

Clay paving bricks

Clay bricks used for paving are the same sizes as ordinary bricks, but they are harder and denser than the type of brick usually used for building construction, while clay brick pavers are similar in appearance when laid but are controlled by a different British Standard. Paving bricks are made to the same dimensions as ordinary building bricks (215 x 102.5 x 65 mm) and they should be not less than type FL (Frost resistant and Low soluble salt content) as specified in BS 3921, and they should be solid bricks without perforations or frogs. Engineering bricks to BS 3921, which are extremely strong and durable, are the best of all paving bricks, but they are made only in monotone red or dark grey/blue colours, which give the paving a feeling of permanence and heaviness. This may suit the landscape design if a massive appearance is desirable, but as they are very expensive they may have to be used sparingly.

The alternative to clay brick paving is to use calcium silicate bricks; being a man-made material, calcium silicate bricks are somewhat more monotone than clay bricks and are made in lighter shades of yellow, buff and grey. They should be not less than Class 4, which have a strength of 27.5 N/mm^2 as specified in BS 187.

Clay brick pavers

The difference today between paving bricks and brick pavers is mainly one of size and shape. Historically pavers were much harder and stronger clay units (usually dark blue with a raised square or diamond pattern) designed for use in stables, goods yards, and other places where iron tyred wheels and the shoes of heavy horses imposed the need for a very hard-wearing surface. The impact of four three-quarter ton horses swinging a four ton loaded iron-tyred cart round a yard would destroy anything but the hardest granite or clay paving. Rubber tyres, however heavily loaded, do not have the same crushing and chipping effects as iron tyres, though they can eventually wear the naturally rough surface down.

Clay brick pavers are controlled by BS 6677: Part 1 which specifies two types; PA which is suitable for pedestrian areas, driveways and casual car parking only, and PB which is suitable for roads and heavy commercial vehicles. Both types have to comply with standards of skid-resistance. Pavers are made in thicknesses of 50 mm and 65 mm; the 50 mm pavers are best used for foot traffic, while the 65 mm pavers are suitable for vehicles. Pavers are made in a similar way to paving bricks, but they are made in a wider range of sizes:

        215 x 102.5 x 65 mm thick
        215 x 102.5 x 50 mm
        210 x 105   x 65 mm
        210 x 105   x 50 mm
        200 x 100   x 65 mm
        200 x 100   x 50 mm

Paving bonds

Where vehicles are likely to run on the paving, both paving bricks and pavers must be locked together to prevent the wheels of turning or skidding vehicles from spreading them apart. There are many possible patterns of laying (or 'bonds') which help to lock the pavers together; one of the most common is 'herring-bone', that is, rectangular blocks laid in V-shaped patterns.

For pedestrian-only areas where only occasional machinery may drive over the paving, a non-locking bond may be used, giving the landscape designer more choice as to the effect of the paving pattern. These are similar to the concrete block patterns described in Section 3.2:

- 'stack bond': straight joints in both directions;
- 'half-bond': straight joints one way, staggered joints the other way;
- 'quarter-bond' as half-bond but smaller stagger;
- 'basket-weave' two bricks laid one way, two laid the other way (this needs a 10 mm joint which may not fit the paving design).

Specially shaped bricks, known as 'specials', are made for infill edging to patterns, kerbs, drainage channels, circular work and for filling manhole covers to match the paving. When the landscape designer is fortunate enough to have a prestigious contract, a manufacturer will produce 'special specials' which can be made to an individual design, incorporating a logo or symbol, though much can be achieved by the imaginative use of standard bricks. Some manufacturers are producing shaped interlocking brick pavers which have the same stability as interlocking concrete blocks, which makes them suitable for vehicle overrun areas provided that the pavers are strong enough to carry the weight of the vehicles without crushing. Ordinary building bricks may be cut quite well with hammer and bolster, but the much harder paving bricks will shatter, and where bricks must be cut to finish a pattern, diamond disc power saws should be used, not concrete block cutters or hammer and bolster. If possible, the landscape designer should lay out the paving so as to minimize the number of cut blocks, and if the plans are drawn with a tolerance on the paving dimensions, the paving contractor will be able to use specials or whole bricks rather than cut bricks at edges and junctions. Some details of edging to brick paving are shown in Figure 3.8.

Sub-bases for paving bricks and brick pavers

Brick paving may be laid on a concrete sub-base and bedded in mortar, or laid on a granular sub-base and bedded in sand. A granular sub-base should be designed as for concrete blocks, but for good quality construction where vehicles may use the paving a 'capping layer' of well-rammed hardcore should be laid on the sub-grade below the sub-base; this is then called an 'improved sub-grade'. If the CBR is between 2 and 5 per cent a capping layer of 300 mm is needed; between 1 and 2 per cent a 600 mm capping layer; while if the CBR is below 1 per cent, hand the design of the sub-base over to a highway engineer; there are problems! The design of sub-bases is described in greater detail in Section 1.1.

A solid concrete sub-base, used only where bricks are to be bedded in mortar, should be not less than 300 mm thick for pedestrian areas, laid on a consolidated sub-strate. Alternatively, a 100–150 mm concrete sub-base may be laid on a well-rammed hardcore capping layer which is blinded with sand, and the concrete may need to be reinforced if the sub-strate is unsound, or if there is likely to be vehicle overrun. Any pockets of weak ground should be dug out and filled with well-rammed hardcore or weak concrete before the sub-base is laid. Remember that even if the final paving is intended to be free from vehicles, the contractor's oil-dripping trucks are quite probably going to drive over the area in order to dump loads or bring the foreman's tea, so it is advisable to leave the final paving as late as possible in the contract and to make good any damage in the sub-base or base layers before the paving units are laid.

Bedding and jointing brick paving

The bedding and jointing of paving is described in greater detail in Bedding and Jointing Generally (pages 42–43). Brick paving may be laid either in a lime:sand mortar bed, or dry-bedded in sand in a similar way to concrete blocks. Lime:sand mortar is not easily mixed satisfactorily on site, and is therefore usually supplied ready-mixed. Bricks, like other small unit paving, can become hazards if they are not laid level. The tolerances on good quality brick paving are:

finished surface variation from the designed level $= \pm 6$ mm
variation between two adjoining bricks $\qquad = \pm 2$ mm
variation over 3000 mm in any direction $\qquad = \pm 10$ mm

The laying of brick pavers and paving bricks is shown in Figure 3.8.

Mortar bedding is used for slopes steeper than 1 in 10, edging, drainage channels, ramps, and areas where things are going to be dropped or thrown (pub beer cask loading), or where the paving is likely to be continuously wet. The sub-base must be concrete, as granular sub-bases are too flexible to support rigidly bedded units. The bed should be 20 mm thick of $1:\frac{1}{4}:3$ or 4 cement:lime:sand mortar, using BS 882 Grade M sand, and plasticizers should not be permitted. The jointing is usually done as the work proceeds, and the joints are struck flush to avoid any chance of water collecting in the joints. Movement joints are needed every 6000 mm or at changes of direction, and next to rigidly constructed manholes. It is also important to remember that wherever there is a movement joint in the sub-base this must be matched by the movement joint in the paving. Movement joints are usually 10 mm wide, constructed of solid polyethylene foam, or a flexible two-part polysulphide sealant to BS 4254, or a silicone sealant to

BS 5889. (These two standards are obsolescent but have not yet been replaced.)

Recommendations for laying sand-bedded paving are given in BS 6677: Part 2, *Code of Practice for Design of Lightly Trafficked Pavements*. In sand bedding on a granular sub-base, the same principles apply to bedding brick paving as those for concrete blocks, but some manufacturers consider that a 30 mm compacted bedding sand layer is better than the 50 mm recommended for concrete blocks. The edge restraint should be constructed before the paving is laid, but because it is not very easy to lay a large area of pavers exactly to a given dimension, it is preferable to put in a temporary timber edging of boards supported by posts and to lay the final edging afterwards. The bedding sand is laid loose to 30 mm thickness and compacted, then a thin layer of loose sand is spread on this bed on which the brick paving is laid. Dry sand is brushed into the joints, and the paving is then compacted with a vibrating plate compactor. The paving should then have another treatment which consists of brushing sand into the joints and compacting, followed by a final brushing in of sand.

Frost, oil, petrol, sharp metal, paint, cement and bitumen are all enemies to brick paving – indeed to paving of any kind – and if the paving must be laid at an early stage of the contract, protective plywood sheets (not just torn old polythene) or the proper insulating mats used for curing concrete should be laid on top until all danger of damage is past. However much the contractor assures the landscape designer that all damage will be made good, paving that has been ripped up and replaced never looks quite as smooth and elegant as undisturbed paving.

Repairs

As with all small paving units, it is difficult to replace them perfectly after they have been lifted for the repair of service runs, and it is advisable to lay a strip of flags over the service run to make replacement easier. A further advantage of this method is that after a number of years it is very unlikely that the contractor will have matching bricks, and an area patched with variegated bricks will look worse than a neat line of flags. If the cost limits can be bent slightly, special paving units can be made with 'GAS', 'WATER' or 'ELECTRIC' moulded into them and laid to mark the service run. In new work it may be possible to persuade the services engineers to run their services in a position which allows a line of flags to be fitted into the paving pattern. A list of the services which may disrupt paving is given in the section on manholes in Chapter 6, Drainage. It is a good idea to make the path wider than necessary so that the service runs can be kept to one side, where the usual little piles of old concrete, broken shovels, and decrepit striped tape always found on maintenance jobs, will not be a hazard.

3.6 COBBLES

Cobbles are large sea-smoothed stones obtained from geologically old beaches, many of which are now miles from the sea on raised beaches. The collection of cobbles is firmly controlled by the environmental authorities, as the shingle beaches which contain the best cobbles are often legally protected geological features such as Dungeness or Chesil Bank. One of the tenderers for the Channel Tunnel proposed to get the material for concreting by excavating Dungeness, which is an internationally protected site, and it will not surprise the landscape designer to learn that the contract went to another firm. The environmentally conscious specifier should therefore make sure that the proposed source of cobbles or shingle is unimpeachable.

Since cobbles are expensive to buy, and still more expensive to lay, they are usually used only for small decorative paved areas, or as dividing strips at awkward junctions. Except for the very small sizes – under 50 mm – they are not comfortable to walk on, and even then they should never be used where disabled or elderly people will walk. Cobbles must always be set in concrete, as loose cobbles are historically the ammunition of rebels and rioters, and nowadays of vandals, car-thieves, and shop-raiders. The smaller stones go well in catapults, while the larger ones can be used very effectively by baseball players and cricketers. Although cobbles are rounded, they can still trap small pieces of litter such as cigarette butts and lolly sticks, so they are better suited to small private pathways and ornamental paving.

Cobble types

Cobbles come in a wide range of colours, depending on their mother rock, including pale grey, dark grey, pink, brown, sandy buff, cream, blue-green, and speckled, patchy, or striped. They are measured by the sieve size passed. The range given here is typical of the sizes and colours of cobbles:

- South Coast flint origin cobbles, grey or sandy, 100 to 75 mm, 75 to 50 mm, and 50 to 40 mm.
- Norfolk cobbles, dark grey, 100 to 75 mm.
- Cumbrian granite cobbles, dark grey, pink and brown mixed, over 100 mm, 100 to 75 mm, 75 to 50 mm, 50 to 20 mm.
- Scottish granite, gneiss and quartz mixed, light pink-brown speckled and banded, over 100 mm, 100 to 75 mm, 75 to 50 mm, 50 to 30 mm.
- Scottish granite, light grey and light brown, 450 to 300 mm, 300 to 150 mm.
- Shropshire quartzite, red-brown, 150 to 100 mm, 125 to 50 mm, 75 to 50 mm.

Sub-bases and bedding for cobbles

Cobbles are usually laid on a BS 5328 Standard Mix ST1 concrete base and bedded in stiff 1:3 cement:sand mortar. The bed will obviously vary considerably according to the size and shape of the cobbles, but the minimum thickness should be 25 mm. The bedding is laid over a small section of the work and the cobbles pressed down into it one by one; the cobbles are tapped home with a wooden maul,

Plate 16 *Traditional cobble paving separating the grass from the flagged path. Note the pleasant swirling pattern around the tree; a subtle but effective use of cobbles.*

and finally dry-grouted with 1:3 cement:sand grout. This grout is then lightly watered with a fine spray watering can – not a hose – to settle the grout in so that it finishes within 15 to 20 mm of the top surface. It may be preferable to use white or coloured cement to set off the cobbles, and it is essential to see that the grout is neither watered too little so that the bottom of the joint does not set, or watered too much so that the grout is washed out. The watering must be very gentle to avoid cement being washed up the sides of the cobbles, and if heavy rain is forecast the finished work must be protected. If the cobbles are laid on a slope, the lower

75

courses must be laid first in a rather stiff mortar, and no more than five or six rows should be laid at one time, otherwise the whole paving may tilt downwards or even slide downhill. Edge restraint is necessary for cobbles which do not abut hard paving, and any edging or kerb will be suitable as long as it is compatible with the design.

Cobble laying is a skilled job, and the landscape designer should make sure that the contractor has a reliable paviour with experience of cobble laying. The points to look for in good cobble paving are: all stones the same height, all bedded to the same depth, no smears of grout on the exposed part of the stones, and as cobbles are seldom quite round, the flatter faces should all be set in the same direction, preferably in the direction of the drainage fall. Really good cobble paving is laid in sweeps which give a patterned appearance that can be used to lead the eye towards a focal point such as a specimen tree or entrance, while badly laid cobbles look as though they had been flung down at random. A sample panel should be approved by the landscape designer before the main work is carried out.

3.7 GRASS CONCRETE

Grass concrete is the name given to proprietary in situ or precast concrete units which are perforated to allow grass to be grown in the open sections. Included under this heading are the plastic units which fulfil the same purpose but which are not so robust. There is no British Standard for grass concrete, so the landscape designer will have to rely on the manufacturer's claims as to its suitability for the job. The percentage of open section to solid ranges from 50 to 80 per cent; the more open blocks are used for pedestrian areas, occasional overspill car parking, tree grilles and individual house driveways so that the concrete is almost invisible under the grass. The more solid blocks are designed for frequent car parking, embankments, ditch lining, and fire paths in grassed areas where the concrete sections are more apparent. Although the paving is called 'grass' concrete, the open sections may equally well be filled with well-rammed hoggin or bound gravel, which is less likely to wear into pits and ruts than plain hoggin or gravel and is more resistant to wear than grass (see Figure 3.9).

Fire paths
Grass concrete is very often used for 'fire paths' at the back of buildings, where (hopefully) only occasional access for emergency vehicles is necessary. Fire engines are the largest and heaviest emergency vehicles that will need access and it is therefore for them that these paths must be designed as they need the correct size and strength of roadway if they are to operate properly, and fire engines working on very high buildings can weigh up to 42 tonnes. When specifying grass concrete the manufacturer must be informed of the load the product will have to carry, and the correct sub-base should be carefully specified. The local fire brigade should also

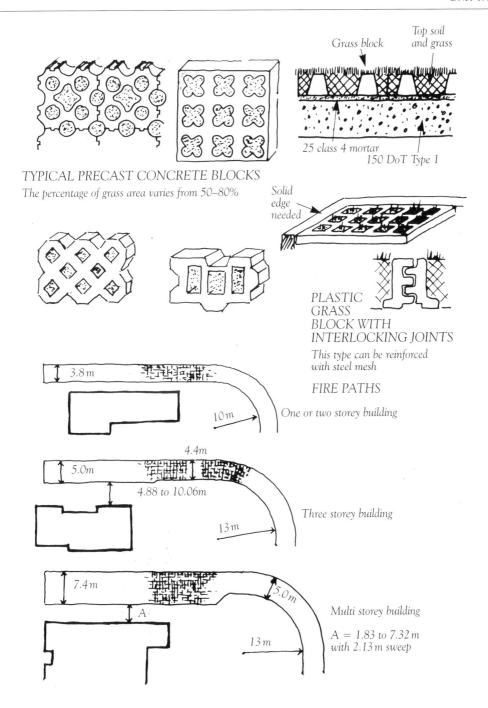

TYPICAL PRECAST CONCRETE BLOCKS

The percentage of grass area varies from 50–80%

Grass block

Top soil and grass

25 class 4 mortar

150 DoT Type 1

Solid edge needed

PLASTIC GRASS BLOCK WITH INTERLOCKING JOINTS

This type can be reinforced with steel mesh

FIRE PATHS

3.8 m

10 m

One or two storey building

5.0 m

4.4m

4.88 to 10.06m

13 m

Three storey building

7.4 m

A

5.0 m

13 m

Multi storey building

A = 1.83 to 7.32 m
with 2.13 m sweep

Figure 3.9   Grass concrete

77

be consulted. Fire paths should be marked out by signs since with very successful grassing the position of the path may be concealed by the lush growth, especially if the mowing regime has suffered from an economical grounds manager. The requirements for fire paths are set out below and are shown in Figure 3.9.

- one or two storeys: 3.8 m road, 3.8 m working point, 10 m inside turning radius;
- three storeys: 4.4 m road, 5.0 m working point, 13 m inside turning radius;
- multi-storey: 5.0 m road, 7.4 m working point, 13 m inside turning radius;

Precast concrete units

Precast concrete is the most commonly used material for grass concrete paving. The foundation for this paving must be permeable to allow water to reach the grass roots, and surplus water to drain away easily, so either ballast, hardcore, or any other free-draining granular material should be laid under the sub-base if the natural ground is impervious clay. The size and thickness of the blocks available range from small thick units about 400 x 400 x 150 mm thick to large thin units about 600 x 600 x 75 mm thick. Many of these units may be supplied reinforced with light steel mesh for use in areas where point loads would fracture plain concrete blocks. It is therefore important that the manufacturer is given the fullest information about the proposed use of the paving. Grass concrete blocks may be plain rectangular, hexagonal, or interlocking (mostly used for embankments) and are made in several thicknesses for different loadings.

Plastic units

There are two types available; reinforced plastic blocks similar to concrete but larger and lighter, and in situ construction using a plastic former filled with concrete on site. As both these systems depend very much on good workmanship they are supplied and installed by specialist contractors. The plastic blocks are thinner and larger than concrete blocks, about 900 x 300 x 30 mm or 50 mm thick, and with a very much higher proportion of open to solid sections. They are laid in much the same way as concrete blocks, though some manufacturers recommend laying a 50 mm layer of fertile soil/sand mix below the blocks to allow the grass to root firmly. Because of the thin fins between sections, they can also be filled with industrial turf laid over the blocks and rolled in. This is a less sturdy method and is best used for light work.

In situ grass concrete is constructed by laying a plastic former reinforced with steel mesh over the ground; these are then filled with air-entrained concrete and levelled off. When the concrete has set, the exposed part of the former is burned off, and the resulting voids filled with soil and seeded as for concrete blocks. The requirements for sub-bases, blinding with soil/sand mix, and seeding are the same as for other types of block, but an edge restraint is needed for in situ grass concrete. Landscape designers should note that the burning-out process can be obnoxious, and it is probably better not to specify this type for large grass concrete areas close to occupied buildings. The advantage of in situ grass concrete is that steel reinforcement can be incorporated into the path to make it capable of supporting greater loads without deformation. Details of grass concrete bedding are shown in Figure 3.9.

Sub-bases for grass concrete

The sub-base should be Type 1 granular material, laid on a free-draining sub-strate or if the sub-strate is water-retaining, land drainage must be installed to allow the grass to form a proper sward. There is normally no need to provide surface water drainage, as the paving is perforated. A minimum thickness of 150 mm sub-base is satisfactory for pedestrians and light traffic, but where heavier traffic or commercial vehicles are expected the CBR should be checked and the rules for designing the sub-base should be followed as described in Section 1.1. If the sub-strate is very soft, it may be advisable to lay a geotextile fabric under the sub-base to prevent mud from percolating into the sub-base. As edging is not usually used for grass concrete, the sub-base should extend about 500 mm each side of the blocks to stop them subsiding into the sub-strate.

Bedding and filling grass concrete precast blocks

The concrete blocks should be laid about 20 mm below any existing adjoining grass so that there is no risk of the mower catching the edge of the blocks; if the adjoining grass is newly turfed or sown a further 15 mm should be allowed for settlement since the blocks which are on a firm sub-base will settle less than the neighbouring topsoil. The sub-base is covered with a 20 mm layer of fine dry sand, and the blocks are bedded in this. They are not vibrated, but should be tapped into place with a wooden maul so as to leave not more than 3 mm difference in level between adjoining blocks; and unlike solid concrete blocks they do not need to be laid to falls. The blocks are then filled with fine sifted good quality topsoil, with any necessary pre-seeding fertilizers and weedkillers incorporated, and seeded with a suitable grass mixture. Grass concrete manufacturers usually supply their own special seed mixes which they consider to be best suited to their product; typical mixes would be:

● For pedestrians and light car parking:

   20 per cent chewings fescue
   20 per cent smoothstalked meadow grass
   25 per cent perennial ryegrass
   25 per cent creeping red fescue
   10 per cent browntop.

● For fire paths and service areas:

   25 per cent chewings fescue
   35 per cent creeping red fescue
   15 per cent smoothstalked meadow grass
   15 per cent perennial ryegrass
   10 per cent browntop.

Grass concrete needs more care than ordinary grassed areas during the contract maintenance period as the seeding or turf is more susceptible to drying out, and allowance for extra watering in dry weather should be included in the specification. Normal maintenance mowing can be carried out as for ordinary grassed areas, but it is advisable to check the level of the soil filling and to top it up well during the maintenance period, since some soil pockets may settle more than others, leaving projecting edges to trip pedestrians and ruin mower blades. Soil above the blocks causes no problems, but soil below the blocks is a particular hazard since the projecting edges are hidden by the grass.

3.8 PEDESTRIAN DETERRENT PAVING

This could equally well be called car deterrent paving, since it is very useful for discouraging illegal parking without the need to erect a visual barrier. The name encompasses any type of unit paving with units deliberately designed to be very uncomfortable or even impossible for walking or driving; they are laid where pedestrians or cars must be kept off, but where prickly planting, fences or walls are not suitable barriers. Though ordinary deterrent paving is good enough to deter mildly lawless intruders, it can be crossed by determined dumper trucks, dogs, wild bikers, ram-raiders and urban vandals, either because they see it as a challenge, or because they don't mind it, and heavier barriers than deterrent paving are needed for controlling these intruders.

Advantages

Typical areas where pedestrian deterrent paving is used are islands in roads where sight lines must be maintained but where people must not get too near the traffic; tempting illegal parking places outside buildings, and restricted areas where pedestrians should not go in country parks, superstores and nature reserves. Such paving is useful for keeping people away from windows in medical premises, banks, schools, health clubs and other places where 'peering in' should be discouraged, or where open casement windows can be a hazard to passers-by. Although deterrent paving will not stop burglars, it is difficult to run across, and can be usefully used to make escape routes hazardous for intruders. Used in conjunction with grass concrete, pedestrian deterrent paving can control careless car parking and prohibited short cuts very satisfactorily without the need for visual barriers. Quite a narrow strip of such paving will stop short-cuts across grassed areas. It also has the advantage that fire engines or cross country emergency vehicles can be driven across it in an emergency and therefore the crews do not need to have gate keys for access to casualties.

Disadvantages

The disadvantage of deterrent paving is its ability to trap litter, but there are some types of paving on the market which consist of pyramidal or rounded units; these can be cleaned or washed fairly easily.

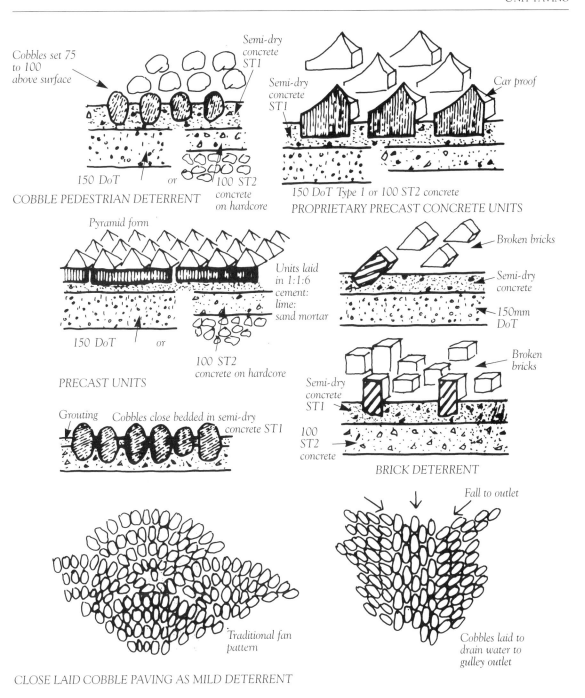

Cobbles set 75 to 100 above surface

Semi-dry concrete ST1

Car proof

Semi-dry concrete ST1

150 DoT or 100 ST2 concrete on hardcore

COBBLE PEDESTRIAN DETERRENT

150 DoT Type 1 or 100 ST2 concrete

PROPRIETARY PRECAST CONCRETE UNITS

Pyramid form

Units laid in 1:1:6 cement: lime: sand mortar

150 DoT or 100 ST2 concrete on hardcore

PRECAST UNITS

Broken bricks

Semi-dry concrete

150mm DoT

Grouting

Cobbles close bedded in semi-dry concrete ST1

Semi-dry concrete ST1

100 ST2 concrete

Broken bricks

BRICK DETERRENT

Fall to outlet

Traditional fan pattern

Cobbles laid to drain water to gulley outlet

CLOSE LAID COBBLE PAVING AS MILD DETERRENT

Figure 3.10   Deterrent paving

Deterrent paving units

Most deterrent paving is constructed from special units, but standard concrete blocks or brick pavers set at an angle work quite well, though their projection above ground is less than that of the purpose made units. Both purpose made units and standard units must be hand-bedded in concrete on a granular sub-base in the same way as for cobbles, as neither rollers nor vibrating plates can be used to finish the surface. Cobbles themselves provide a deterrent surface, though being rounded they are not as painful to walk on as the angular blocks. Concrete units can be finished in any of the same materials as ordinary paving; exposed aggregate, textured concrete, or coloured to form patterns. Gaps in the paving may be left for planting, but it is as well to place these within reach of a smooth access path, or the plants are likely to be left unwatered and unweeded if it is too painful to get to them. Deterrent paving may help to keep vandals away from young trees in urban areas, and although the paving can be crossed by determined vandals, most tree damage is caused by casual passers-by rather than by deliberate attackers. Typical deterrent paving units are illustrated in Figure 3.10.

Manholes and other access covers should be sited clear of deterrent paving if

Plate 17 *A successful example of bold pedestrian and car deterrent paving units with a sculptural appearance.*

Plate 18 *These pedestrian deterrent units could have been kept clean and weedfree with little trouble; if the client is not prepared to carry out regular maintenance they will eventually look like grass concrete.*

possible; if access covers must be placed in the paving there should be a clear flat surface at least 600 mm wide all round the cover so that workmen do not have to stand on the deterrent paving. As with all other decorative paving units, disturbance to the surface for maintenance and repairs always leaves traces, however carefully the work is done; therefore service runs should be located clear of the paving if possible. If runs must pass under the paving, it is advisable to mark them with a line of flat brick or concrete units which can be lifted and replaced without disturbing the main paving.

The ultimate in deterrent paving – if it can be called that – is the concrete ditch used round high security areas where the theft of vehicles or ram-raiding is a risk. This is a ditch made of half-round concrete pipes at least 1 m diameter and 500 mm deep, which will trap the wheels of even large trucks, and can only be crossed by tracked vehicles. Half-round sections of precast concrete solid or perforated soakaway pipes are suitable, but drainage must be provided to remove surface water. The ditch must be protected on the public side by a raised kerb, preferably a high vehicular kerb of the type used in lorry parks and motorways, and a guard rail to prevent pedestrians from falling in; they should also be well lit.

4 GRANULAR PAVING

This section covers loose materials such as natural aggregate, gravel, hoggin, shale (blaes) and shingle paving (though not cobbles which are set in concrete; these are described in Chapter 3, Unit Paving). There are also a number of artificially coloured concrete or natural aggregates available which can be had in bright red, orange, blue or vivid green, all sealed with epoxy resin, but these are not discussed as their appearance is unlikely to appeal to the landscape designer and their life expectancy is not fully established. It is a point of good design to use a material native to the area for countryside projects unless there is good reason for using contrasting materials. A note on bark paths is also included in this chapter, as there is an increasing demand for bark or woodchip surfaced paths for rural projects. The most common use for granular materials is as an ornamental surround for boulder groups, specimen trees, grave dressing, garden show paths, rock or scree gardens and planter covering, but these cannot be classified as paving and are not included in this book. Courtyard paving may be considered as ornamental or practical depending on the amount of access to the court, but it is advisable to design court paving with proper bases in case the usage changes (see Figure 4.1).

The construction of granular paving is simple compared with unit or monolithic paving; the top surface of chosen material is laid on a base and a sub-base, provided with an edging, then raked to falls and rolled. Apart from bound gravel and hoggin which can be compacted into a firm surface, granular paving materials never set into a hard-wearing permanent surface, but remain in a semi-flexible state and therefore none of them are satisfactory for regular vehicular traffic. Unlike unit paving or monolithic paving, granular paving itself is a permeable material, and therefore does not require drainage apart from providing adequate falls and cambers to throw off heavy rainfall, though if the sub-strate is impermeable it may be necessary to provide sub-strate drainage to prevent the surface from becoming waterlogged. The thickness of the base in soils with various water-table levels is given in Table 4.1. Because of its flexible nature, granular paving requires regular maintenance to keep it in good condition. It should be noted that some gravels and aggregates can produce run-off water which is strongly alkaline or acid, and if the planting adjoining the gravelled area has

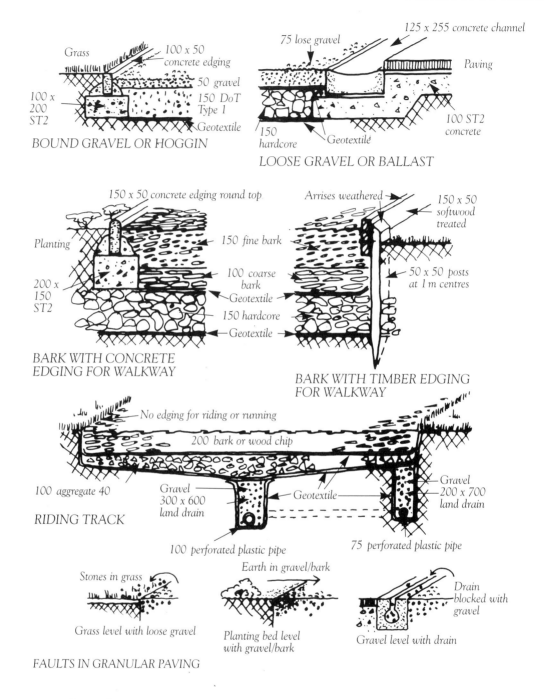

Figure 4.1 Granular Paving

definite pH requirements the gravel must be chosen accordingly or an inert material specified.

The advantages of granular paving are:

- low cost compared with unit paving;
- informal appearance, making it suitable for informal landscapes;
- easy maintenance by unskilled manual labour, provided that replacement material is readily available;
- easily adapted to irregular shapes such as serpentine paths, circular surrounds to fountains or planted areas;
- no surface water drainage system required except where the sub-strate is impermeable;
- wide range of natural materials with colours and textures which are permanent, though some of the brighter materials will weather naturally as they would do in their place of origin.

The disadvantages of granular paving are:

- they are difficult surfaces (if not impossible) for wheel chair users, prams, trolleys and disabled people generally, as the softer surface induces a feeling of instability and sticks can penetrate the surface;
- easily disturbed by heavy traffic, impact loads, skidding and slewing vehicles (hoggin and the self-binding gravels are less easily damaged);
- they are not practicable on steep slopes as the material tends to get washed and trodden downhill;
- regular maintenance is absolutely essential if ponding, ruts and pits are not to occur – even light pedestrian traffic will eventually wear holes in a granular surface;
- a regular programme of weed control is needed to keep the paving looking smart and to prevent soil formation by weed roots;
- leaf and litter sweeping must be done carefully to avoid removing the surface material;
- an edging must always be provided to contain the material, though this need not necessarily be considered a disadvantage;
- loose gravel or rock aggregate can cause grazing to exposed flesh and can be thrown about by vandals.

Figure 4.1 shows typical granular paving construction details.

Bases and sub-bases

Because of its unstable nature, the base for granular paving is of great importance, and because it is usually laid by unskilled labour the base layers are inclined to be treated casually unless careful site supervision is provided. The bearing capacity of the sub-strate at formation level must be checked, and any weak spots must be excavated and filled with well-rammed base material. A total herbicide should be applied to the sub-strate where plant or seed material is likely to be present in the ground at formation level. The sub-strate must be correctly levelled before the base layer is laid, as a variable base layer can lead to uneven subsidence.

All final levelling must be done on the base layers. The materials used for the base must be permeable in order to allow the water which will drain through the surfacing to pass through the base for dispersal or collection into a surface water drain. Water which is trapped between the surfacing and the base will carry loose material with it as it drains away. The base material should be free from any deleterious material or contaminants such as earth, oil, building chemicals, or organic matter. The base should be laid and rolled in layers not exceeding 150 mm, and after laying the base should be given a light rolling which is sufficient for residential paths and ornamental areas; heavier rolling is preferable for public pedestrian areas.

No site traffic should be allowed on the base after it has been levelled. The contractor should not be permitted to store material such as fuel oil or building chemicals on the areas to be surfaced, as these may leach into the base and affect the finished surface. Exposed bases or finishes may be subject to frost-heave and must be re-compacted after periods of frost.

The thickness of the base depends on the bearing capacity of the ground at formation level. Granular paving is not suitable for heavy traffic, and full-scale road bases are therefore not necessary, but where vehicle overrun is absolutely unavoidable the sub-base must be calculated as described in Section 1.1. A simplified version of the *Department of Transport Road Note 29, Soil Loading Applicable to Light Surfacings* is given below. If the water table is less than 600 mm below formation level subsoil drainage should be provided.

The material used for the base must be granular material Type 1 or Type 2 free from deleterious material and dust, well graded, and pass a 75 mm BS sieve. It must not be susceptible to frost action as most of the base will be above the normal frost

Table 4.1
Approximate thickness of base for British soils

Soil type	Water table > 600 mm below formation level (mm)	Water table < 600 mm below formation level (mm)
Heavy clay	180–230	230–380
Silty clay	140	180
Sandy clay	100–120	140–160
Sand poorly graded	100	100
Sand well graded	100	100
Well graded sandy gravel	100	100

free level which is accepted as being 500 mm below ground. It should consist of clean hard inert material such as:

- crushed hard rock;
- quarry scalpings;
- crushed concrete;
- crushed hard well burnt brick;
- gravel;
- blastfurnace slag (not steelmaking slag);
- approved mining waste.

The pH of the material should be checked, as water can permeate the surface and carry groundwater of an acid or alkaline nature to the adjoining planting. If the base material is open in texture it is usual to 'blind' the base. The purpose of blinding the base is to fill the interstices of the base in order to form a perfectly graded layer on which to lay the surfacing. The sand should be either to BS 882 Grade C or M, or other clean well graded sand if samples are approved by the landscape designer, and it should be compacted by plate vibrator.

Geotextiles and filter fabrics

There are a number of British Standard methods of testing for geotextiles, but these are concerned with the material itself and do not give recommendations for use on site. The main functions of geotextiles in granular paving are the following:

- To maintain the separate layers of the paving. Unless the sub-strate contains no fine particles, it is advisable to lay a geotextile filter layer between the sub-strate and the base to prevent mud or fine sand from percolating upwards into the base.
- To prevent the base and the surfacing material mixing if the surfacing contains fine particles. The action of wheels on granular materials can produce a churning movement which mixes the material from the top and bottom layers together; this must be prevented by a geotextile separating layer.
- To provide a drainage layer to remove surface water from the paving, as a waterlogged granular paving loses much of its strength and cohesiveness.
- To distribute loads on the paving evenly over the surface in order to avoid point loads 'punching through' the top layer. This is particularly important where wheels must always run along the same track because of the narrowness of the paving; even light machine wheels will wear ruts in time.

Geotextiles are manufactured in a range of textures which offer greater or lesser permeability to water, usually expressed as ratio of voids to solids. Sand has a ratio of voids to solids ranging from 0.4:1 to 0.8:1, cohesive soils 0.5:1 to 3:1, while geotextiles have a ratio of 5:1 up to 10:1 or more. This allows the landscape designer to select a geotextile which has greater drainage properties than the paving material so that water will always be removed from the surface.

There is a conflict between the need to provide an open-textured geotextile with good drainage properties and the need to provide a strong close-textured fabric which will stand up to loading, and the landscape designer should consult the manufacturer before selecting a geotextile. A good geotextile must be puncture resistant, tear resistant, proof against UV light (while being laid), resistant to chemicals in the range pH 2 to pH 13, and not likely to stretch or shrink, though still elastic enough to accommodate small irregularities under 100 mm in the base layer. Rolls are joined by sewing where stress is expected, but in light work an overlap of 50 mm is adequate if the material is covered as soon as laid. Even light site traffic should not be allowed to run on the geotextile before the top layer is laid on it. Geotextiles should be treated as carefully designed engineering materials and not handled or laid casually.

Drainage of granular surfaces

Although surface water drainage is not normally necessary for granular paving, heavy rain can wash away the surface, and for this reason loose surfacing should not be laid to falls greater than 1:20 cross-fall, and 1:40 longitudinal fall unless guaranteed by the supplier and contractor. Wind force as well can move loose gravel or chippings on very exposed sloping sites, and loose surfacings should not be used even on level areas if heavy surface water or wind scour is likely to occur. If the sub-strate is impermeable, or very slow-draining, it is necessary to install land drainage to ensure that the paving remains dry and sound even in bad weather. The softer materials, especially bark surfaces, can easily degenerate into muddy morasses under heavy use unless the construction is capable of handling continual wet weather and raised ground water levels. Sub-strate or land drainage is discussed in Chapter 6, Drainage of paved areas.

4.1 GRAVEL MATERIALS

Gravel

Gravel is usually taken to mean particles ranging from 5 to 15 mm, consisting of crushed hard rock or natural pebbles. The particles may be all of one size, or evenly graded between given sizes. Gravel is usually specified as fine, medium, or coarse, but each supplier has different definitions of these terms. Gravel should be specified to comply with samples taken from a named pit or other source. It may be specified as river or pit gravel, or as a named rock such as Derbyshire spar in the form of crushed rock aggregate. Pit, beach, or river gravel should be specified as 'washed' to remove salts which would cause efflorescence. Pea gravel is a naturally occurring gravel with even pea sized particles. The spar aggregates can be produced with bright clear colours, but most natural gravel is neutral coloured in the brown-grey range.

Crushed rock aggregate is composed of crushed and graded natural rock which offers a wide range of colours; some of the commonest rock aggregates are:

- white spar: sparkling white 4–9 mm size, rather hard appearance;
- black spar: sparkling black 4–9 mm, mostly used for ornamental graves (spars come in a very wide range of colours, and they can be blended by the supplier to produce almost any shade required);
- golden quartzite: very warm colour, 8–10 mm size;
- white calcined flint: soft white duller than spar, 3–8 mm;
- Derbyshire spar: white and brown warm colour, 3–8 mm;
- granite chippings: sparkling grey/pink with hard appearance, 10–12 mm.

As these materials are produced mechanically by crushing, they have sharper arrises than natural gravel, and can be compacted to a fairly stable surface; but they are only really satisfactory where very little pedestrian traffic is expected, or for purely ornamental fill. The sizes given are the most suitable for paving, but aggregates can be made to order in any size specified by the landscape designer, though any size larger than 25 mm can be considered as pedestrian deterrent paving. Normal sizes supplied are 12 mm, 10–12 mm, 3–8 mm, and 0–3 mm (a range of 0–3 mm means that fine dust may be included in the gravel). Both loose aggregate and gravel are very noisy to walk on; a disadvantage if children are playing on it and an advantage as a warning of unwelcome visitors.

Natural gravel is a natural material excavated from shallow deposits in river valleys. It is fairly standard planning practice to enforce the restoration of gravel pits to environmentally beneficent uses such as wildfowl lakes, fishing ponds, water recreation and the creation of waterside habitats; the landscape designer therefore need not feel that he is despoiling the countryside by using gravel, unless the habitat destroyed by gravel extraction is of particular value. Some more common gravels are:

- pearl quartz: warm grey/silver, 4–6 mm;
- flint 'pebble-dash': warm brown usually used for coating house walls, 6 mm;
- golden gravel: very warm colour, 6–10 mm;
- Thames pea gravel: a rather duller brown/grey 6–10 mm.

Unlike crushed rock aggregate, natural gravels are rounded and tend to be more easily disturbed than the angular materials; equally they are very easily raked back into their proper levels. A typical gravel path would be constructed of:

- edging of precast concrete, stone or brick on 1:2:4 cement:sand:aggregate concrete foundation and haunching;
- base of 150 mm well consolidated hardcore of well broken brick, stone or concrete;

- (if fine gravel – 5 mm and under – is used the hardcore should be blinded with sand);
- 50 to 75 mm layer of gravel raked to falls not steeper than 1 in 20, then lightly watered after laying and before rolling, but only sufficient water should be applied to stabilize the aggregates; too much water will wash away the fine aggregate, especially on slopes.

A suitable edging detail for a gravel path is shown in Figure 4.1.

Gravel laid on anything but the flattest of ground will tend to creep downhill over the years, and it can be persuaded to stay in place by using a plastic or steel wire mesh just below the surface, or by using a plastic grid similar to that used for grass concrete. In both cases the reinforcement will inevitably show up due to pedestrian wear and storm water, so the cost of regular maintenance must be considered at the design stage. Wire mesh may eventually break and produce jagged wire ends unfavourable to walkers in soft shoes and to small children, while plastic mesh can produce loops of fibre which are excellent foot-catchers. The plastic grid is somewhat safer, but where foot traffic is heavy or the path is on a slope an alternative to loose gravel should be specified.

Self-binding gravels

Where there is a need for more stable gravel paths there are some special gravels which are carefully graded by the producer to give a self-binding finish which can stand much heavier usage than the loose gravels. They are very fine textured with a smooth appearance, and they are available in shades of brown, gold and grey. This paving needs to be laid more carefully than loose gravel, making it somewhat more expensive than ordinary gravel, and the landscape designer should specify that:

- the sub-strate must be carefully graded and soft spots cut out and filled with well-rammed hardcore;
- levels must be formed accurately in the base and not in the surface material;
- the base layer should be free-draining 0–28 mm graded gravel (but for limestone gravels use DoT Type 1 granular fill) 150 mm thick well compacted with a 1 tonne roller;
- the top layer is laid moist, lightly compacted with a 500 kg roller to 50 mm minimum thickness, and then well watered with a fine spray;
- when the surface water has been absorbed, the gravel is rolled again with a 500 kg roller;
- two more watering and rolling operations must be carried out within a week of laying;
- the paving must be carefully maintained for the first three months by regular watering and rolling, and any later damage must be cut out and a full depth patch put in with the same technique as the original paving.

It is also possible to construct paving from gravel or aggregate bonded with resin compounds, but these are comparatively recent and the effects of wear and weather are not fully known. Resin bonding gives a very hard easily cleaned weed-free surface, but much of the natural beauty of the material is lost through the disguise of the resin, and the falls must be designed for the rapid run-off generated by the impervious surface. Such paving should be seen more as an artificial surface than a natural granular paving, and its place in the landscape design needs careful consideration.

4.2 BALLAST, HOGGIN AND SHALE

Ballast
This is a mixture of sand and gravel as dug from the pit. The proportion of sand to gravel may vary, and the ballast should be specified to comply with a sample. The colour ranges from pale yellow to mid-brown. A good ballast compacts to a surface which is suitable for light use, but it is not as good as specially selected self-binding gravel or hoggin, though better than loose gravel. Its use should be confined to areas where traffic is occasional and where alternative routes are provided; country overflow parking, grass concrete block fill, and infill to flagged driveways are practicable uses. Ballast is supplied 'as dug' as it contains a naturally graded mix of fine, medium and coarse aggregates. A typical ballast path would be:

- edging of precast concrete, stone or brick on 1:2:4 cement:sand:aggregate concrete foundation and haunching;
- base of 150 mm well consolidated hardcore of well broken brick, stone or concrete;
- 100 to 150 mm layer of ballast raked to falls not steeper than 1 in 20;
- lightly watered after laying and before rolling, but only sufficient water should be applied to stabilize the aggregates; too much water will wash away the fine aggregate, especially on slopes.

Both hoggin and ballast paths can be compartmented by strips of brick, stone or precast concrete laid across them to prevent creep, and these strips can be laid at an angle to the line of the path so as to direct the surface water to the side of the path. However, paths laid with the correct cambers or cross-falls and falls should not need this precaution.

Hoggin
This is a naturally occurring material composed of well graded gravel in a clay matrix, in proportions which form a hard compact surface when laid and rolled. Clay, sand and gravel mixed on site does not constitute hoggin, and will definitely not provide a satisfactory surface. As with all granular materials, a firm edging

must be constructed before the paving is laid. Good hoggin has a long life if properly drained and weeded, but the supply is variable as pits of suitable material are exhausted or opened, and the landscape designer should make sure that hoggin is available locally at a reasonable price before completing the specification. A typical hoggin path would be constructed of:

- edging of precast concrete, stone or brick on 1:2:4 cement:sand:aggregate concrete foundation and haunching;
- base of 150 mm well consolidated hardcore of well broken brick, stone or concrete;
- 100 to 150 mm layer of hoggin raked to falls not steeper than 1 in 20;
- lightly watered after laying and before rolling, but only sufficient water should be applied to stabilize the hoggin.

Shale or blaes

This is mine waste, now no longer produced, but still available in quantity from mine dumps. It is obtainable mainly in the south of Scotland, and forms a useful economical surface for hard playgrounds and small parking areas, though like all loose surfacing it can be rutted and pitted by vehicles or heavy wear. It is a bright reddish coloured material composed of graded particles which when crushed and rolled bind into a firm surface. A disadvantage is that it stains hands and clothes when wet, and can be dusty in dry weather. Shale is specified as:

- edging of precast concrete, stone or brick on 1:2:4 cement:sand:aggregate concrete foundation and haunching;
- base of 150 mm well consolidated hardcore of well broken brick, stone or concrete;
- bottom layer of coarse shale 75 mm thick raked to falls not steeper than 1 in 20;
- top layer of fine shale 50 mm thick;
- lightly watered after laying and before rolling, but only sufficient water should be applied to stabilize the shale.

4.3 BARK AND WOODCHIPS

These materials are not suitable for paved areas in towns since they have very little ability to withstand heavy usage; nor should they be used adjoining buildings, as fragments of wood are liable to be tracked into the entrance. Their proper place is on rural paths, play areas, informal sports tracks, riding tracks and arenas, golf course tracks, and casual walkways through woodland. Bark and woodchip for surfacing is usually made from conifer bark and waste wood from forestry industries which is shredded, broken, or ground to various sizes and grades. Coarse shredded bark may contain some large wood shreds, and conversely, very finely shredded bark can cause dust. It may have been treated with weedkiller or insecticide according to commercial timber requirements, so it is important that the composition of any such chemical (particularly the dangerous methyl bromide which is used to treat imported timber products) should be checked with the manufacturer if the bark is to be used for children's playgrounds, since small children are apt to pick up and suck many unsuitable things. The manufacturer may be asked to provide a certificate that the product conforms with the Control of Substances Hazardous to Health Regulations. Fine woodchips or shreds can be set on fire by vandals, but the fire does not spread easily and is therefore not a fire hazard, and flakes or large chips are comparatively fire-resistant.

A geotextile filter layer should be provided between the sub-strate and the base where the sub-strate contains fine mud or sand, and a filter layer should also be provided between the base and the bark surfacing. All bark surfaces must be well drained; if the water table is at or above 600 mm below formation level subsoil drainage must be provided. It may be advisable to provide subsoil drainage to bark surfaced areas in any case unless the ground is naturally well drained, as nothing smells or feels worse than soggy or slimy bark. A typical bark path with timber or concrete edging is shown in Figure 4.1. The thickness of the bark varies from 100 mm of fine bark for lightly used paths to 300 mm of coarse bark for riding tracks. A typical bark path for walkers would be constructed of:

- edging of precast concrete, stone or brick on 1:2:4 cement:sand:aggregate concrete foundation and haunching, or
- edging of treated softwood or hardwood board 50 x 150 mm with treated timber pegs 50 x 50 mm at 1 m centres;
- total herbicide if the sub-strate is organic soil;
- geotextile drainage and separation layer;
- base of 150 mm well consolidated hardcore of broken brick, stone or concrete;
- geotextile separating, drainage and load distribution layer;
- bottom layer of 50 to 100 mm coarse bark raked to falls not steeper than 1 in 20;
- top layer of 50 to 200 mm fine bark raked to falls.

Note that edging boards are not provided to running tracks or riding tracks as they can cause tripping and this may be a danger to users. Bark and woodchips are both available in a number of different shapes and sizes; although woodchip is cheaper than bark it does not have the same attractive appearance. Natural bark flakes are 'as cut' but most wood products are broken and crushed which damages the fibres; the material becomes more absorbent making a good play surface, but spoiling the appearance of the wood. It is not worth using expensive natural bark where much foot or horse traffic is expected since the flakes will eventually break down and the appearance of the bark will be spoilt – in a heavily used horse track the bark will eventually become composted with the horse droppings and will have to be replaced regularly. Some of the commonest bark products are the following:

- Selected conifer bark flakes: flattish, rich red colour weathering to silvery brown, rather expensive, often used for ornamental mulches, 20–100 mm graded, laid not less than 50 mm thick, maximum slope 1 in 10, drains well, long-lasting.
- Mixed conifer bark chips of various sizes: fairly expensive, more often used as a decorative mulch, 15–60 mm graded, laid not less than 50 mm thick, maximum slope 1 in 12, drains well, long-lasting.
- Whole wood flakes as they come from the axe with some forest material: cheaper than bark but not easy to walk on, 20–100 mm not graded, laid not less than 75 mm thick, maximum slope 1 in 10, drains well, long-lasting.
- Fine woodchips with some forest material: easier to walk on but not very attractive, 5–25 mm not graded, laid not less than 50 mm thick, maximum slope 1 in 15, adequate drainage, short lived.
- Rough woodchips which contain bits of bark, twigs and pine needles: very economical but not attractive, 1–15 mm not graded and contains dust, laid not less than 50 mm thick, maximum slope 1 in 25, poor drainage, short-lived.
- Wood fibre: which is shredded wood, packing down well and soft enough not to damage mowing machinery, 1–30 mm not graded and contains dust, laid not less than 75 mm thick, maximum slope 1 in 12, adequate drainage, medium life.

The maximum slopes given apply only to small areas (under 100 m^2) where erosion is not critical, but on large slopes the bark may work itself down the hill into a pile. Long-lasting means up to four years with normal usage, but the life of the paving may be extended by regular cleaning and replacement of the top surface with fresh material.

There are also a number of special wood materials which are used for safety play surfaces; these are controlled by BS 5696: Parts 2 and 3, and BS 7188 which set standards for impact, fire resistance and other factors. They are usually described as 'play bark' or 'play chips' and range from plain conifer bark chips to wood shreds which are cheaper but not so attractive. Bark or chips used for playground impact absorbing areas (around swings, slides and climbing apparatus) must be dust free, not less than 300 mm thick, and should be raked daily to prevent material being kicked away. The area should be fenced with dog-proof fencing to prevent contamination.

Manufacturers also offer some materials under the heading of 'walk chips' which are much the same as the play materials but are not so strictly controlled. These are produced in either conifer chips 5–30 mm size, or hardwood 5–30 mm size, and are designed to pack down into a firm surface.

The construction of riding tracks is more complicated, as the heavy point loads from hooves can damage the surface more easily than walking boots or trainers.

Although a central land drain is provided in the track, additional catchwater drains may be needed at one or both sides of the track if the ground is liable to become waterlogged. A typical riding track for all-weather use is shown in Figure 4.1 and should be constructed of:

- track bed 3000 mm wide x 300 mm deep, sub-strate treated with total herbicide, lined with geotextile filter membrane;
- central drain trench 300 mm wide x 600 mm deep, lined with geotextile;
- 100 mm clayware agricultural drain, backfilled with gravel waste or hard granular material, discharging into soakaway or watercourse;
- track backfilled with 100 mm of 50 mm aggregate, covered with geotextile;
- track filled to ground level with 200 mm coarse bark or woodchips.

5 KERBS AND EDGINGS

This section covers the types of precast and natural stone units which contain the edges of paving – kerbs, edgings, channels and mowing stones. Most of these can be used with any type of paving, though some are better suited to one type of paving than another. In very large areas and long roadways, the exact detailing of kerbs and edgings is not critical to the appearance of the landscape, but in small pedestrian areas and public spaces, otherwise well designed paving may be spoilt by clumsy detailing of the edges and junctions. From the practical aspect of landscape construction, a sound knowledge of the types of paving edging and the correct method of installing them will enable the landscape designer to make sure that paving units, vehicles, machines, vegetation, water and people all stay within their proper boundaries. Some edges are intended to be physical barriers to wheeled traffic, some are needed for constructional purposes, while others are only demarcation lines between different surfaces.

Most of the kerb and edge units used in landscape work, and nearly all those used in highway work, are plain grey concrete, but aggregate faced units, coloured concrete and various type of tooled finishes are made by some manufacturers, either as standard units or as part of a paving system. The landscape designer may consider that an attractive edge will enhance the appearance of the paving, but like icebergs, very little of it will be visible when laid, and unless the edge of the paving is a critical part of the hard landscape design, there is no great advantage in specifying an expensive material.

5.1 KERBS

The term 'kerb' describes solid heavy units which are used to contain a roadway or paved area, usually where vehicles are expected to overrun the paving either frequently or occasionally. The function of a kerb is to:

- act as a deterrent to vehicle overrun, but be able to stand up to occasional overrun by heavy vehicles without overturning or subsiding;
- prevent the road surface spreading beyond its boundaries because of hot

weather softening, frost expansion, or heavy traffic loading;
- demarcate the roadway without possible mistake (reflective kerbs);
- separate or demarcate grass or other vegetation from the roadway;
- contain and channel surface water to a drainage system;
- resist damage by road machinery, maintenance machinery or misuse of any kind;
- provide a slip-resistant surface for pedestrians at the edge of roadways;
- accentuate a change in level for safety reasons;
- demarcate types of paving, especially those with different functions, such as disabled and normal car parking.

Modern kerbs are most commonly made of dense precast concrete in varying sizes and shapes, ranging from small units suitable for pedestrian areas which can be laid by hand, to massive units designed to stop lorries which must be lifted by machinery. Kerbs are square in section, rounded, chamfered, or bull-nosed on one or both sides. The range of kerb shapes includes straight and curved units, sloping units designed to provide level cross-overs, perforated units for directing surface

Plate 19   *Traditional heavy granite kerb; this size of kerbstone was quite normal, and was carried and placed by hand.*

water to drainage pipes, and reflective kerbs for directing traffic. There are also a number of special shapes for such purposes as controlling extra heavy vehicles and dealing with storm water.

The traditional kerb was made of natural granite, which is now considered too expensive for most applications, though some areas of high architectural quality may still be maintained with granite kerbs. Old worn kerbs – though it takes many generations to wear down a granite kerb – can be reversed and resurfaced to be used again. Other stone has been used in the past for kerbs, but the slip-resistant and hard wearing properties of granite make it the ideal choice for urban kerbstones. 'Conservation' precast concrete kerbs are made by some firms which give the appearance of granite, and these make an economical substitute for real granite though they are obviously not so hard wearing.

Kerbs to British Standard 7263: Parts 1 and 2

These are the most common kerbs in general use. They are covered by BS 7263, and are normally plain grey concrete, although coloured concrete kerbs may be obtained as a special order (see Figure 5.1). They are very plain in appearance, and are not an asset to ornamental paving, where one of the special designs made by paving firms may be more suitable. Kerbs are often used in conjunction with channel units to provide a smooth water channel at the edge of roadways. The concrete for these is made from Portland cement of various types; ordinary, blastfurnace, sulphate resisting, or PFA (pulverized fuel ash), and sometimes other types of binder. The aggregate may be natural material, blastfurnace slag, or PFA, and the kerb units may be coloured, usually in rather sombre shades of grey, red, buff or brown. Kerbs which have to stand up to heavy vehicles thumping over them are made in hydraulic presses, which give a dense hardwearing unit.

Straight kerbs must be between 450 and 915 mm long – mostly 915 mm – and they come in a range of heights and thicknesses. The choice of kerb depends on the level of resistance to vehicles required and the amount of material to be retained. The smaller units are suitable for lightly trafficked or pedestrian areas, while the bigger ones are usually specified for highways. They are specified as one of the following profiles:

- 150 mm high × 125 mm thick
  bull-nosed BS 7263 Type BN
  half battered BS 7263 Type HB3
- 255 mm high × 125 mm thick
  45 degree splayed BS 7263 Type SP
  half battered BS 7263 Type HB2
- 305 mm high × 150 mm thick
  half battered BS 7263 Type HB1

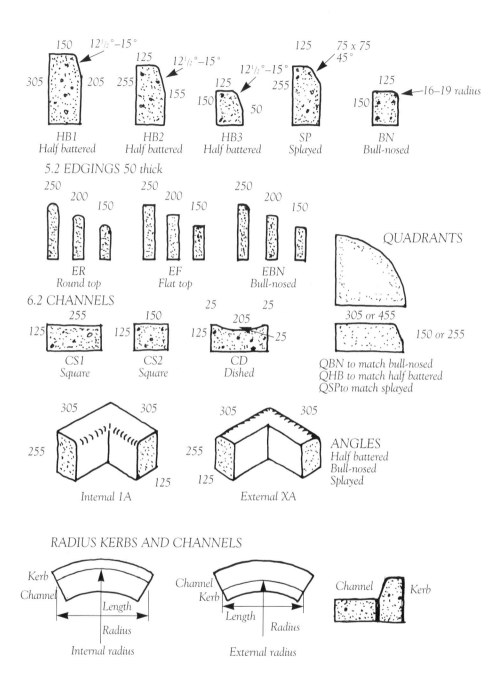

Figure 5.1   Kerbs. British Standard 7263: Part 1

Quadrant kerbs, which are small solid quarter circle kerbs are 150 or 255 mm high, made in the same range of profiles as straight kerbs, and are either 305 or 455 mm radius. They are very useful for turning corners in flag paved areas, as they obviate the need to cut small bits off flags at the corner to fit the curve. They are specified as one of the following profiles:

150 mm high × 305 and 455 mm radius to match type BN	Type QBN
150 mm high × 305 and 455 mm radius to match type HB2, HB3	Type QHB
150 mm high × 305 and 455 mm radius to match type SP	Type QSP
255 mm high × 305 and 455 mm radius to match type BN	Type QBN
255 mm high × 305 and 455 mm radius to match type HB2, HB3	Type QHB
225 mm high × 305 and 455 mm radius to match type SP	Type QSP

Angle kerbs are small L-shaped units designed to provide a very sharp right angle. They are 305 × 305 mm on plan, 225 mm high and 125 mm thick. The profiles match the straight kerbs, and those available are:

● bull-nosed external angle	Type XA
● splayed external angle to match type SP	Type XA
● bull-nosed internal angle	Type IA
● splayed internal angle to match type SP	Type IA

These little units are very useful for making up small tree pit edge units, trimming round manholes or gulleys, making a neat finish to concrete or hoggin under park seats and many similar small jobs which are regrettably often completed by means of the odd bucket of concrete chucked in. Both angle and quadrant kerb units are illustrated in Figure 5.1.

Radial kerbs are designed for gentle curves in roadways, and are the same lengths, heights and profiles as straight kerbs but with a range of radii. The radius and length are measured on the inside of an internal curve, and on the outside of an external curve. This causes complications when designing a serpentine pathway. The units are designed so that a quarter circle can be made with whole units without cutting the kerbs. Radial kerbs are made in all standard profiles of kerbs and channels, so that radial kerbs can be included in the design without changing the profile. Kerbs are supplied to either external or internal radii to suit convex or concave curves respectively (see Figure 5.1).

● External radius: 1.0 m, 2.0 m, 3.0 m, 4.5 m, 6.0 m, 7.5 m, 9.0 m, 10.5 m, 12.0 m
● Internal radius: 3.0 m, 4.5 m, 6.0 m, 7.5 m, 9.0 m, 10.5 m, 12.0 m

Dropper kerbs are shaped to provide a transition between the normal kerb and the crossings which allow vehicles to cross the kerb at road level, such as driveways and entrances to shops and factories. They are made in pairs, right- and left-handed, with profiles which provide a transition from 255 mm high to 150 mm high where the vehicles will cross. A typical dropper kerb crossing is illustrated in Figure 5.2. Standard dropper kerbs are:

- from kerb type HB to BN left handed   type DL1
  right handed   type DR1
- from kerb type SP to BN left handed   type DL2
  right handed   type DR2

Transition kerbs are made to change from one kerb profile to another:

- between type SP and HB left handed   type TL
  right handed   type TR

It is important that the lower edge of dropper kerbs is laid quite flush with the road surface, as wheelchairs are difficult to drive over even small upstands. Where required by the local authority or the client dropper kerb crossings should be marked with tactile slabs to identify them to blind users.

Although the reference codes for individual kerb units are more likely to be the responsibility of the quantity surveyor than that of the landscape designer, it is sensible to be aware of the types and sizes available (see Figure 5.1).

There are situations where heavy impact on the side of the kerb may occur, and special holed kerbs are available for reinforcing with straight steel rods. The rods are 12 mm thick by 150 mm long, set into the foundation below the kerb and inserted into the holes in the kerb, then grouted in as the kerb is bedded. If holed kerbs are not available, or if there is a difficulty in setting out the rods accurately, the steel rods may be set in the haunching behind the kerb, leaving enough room to cover the rod 50 mm all round with the haunching material. Obviously the rods must not project in any direction, as corrosion will soon make them useless, besides being dangerous to users.

Normally water running down the channel at the edge of the roadway is directed into gulleys set in the road, but where this is not feasible 'weir kerbs' may be used which have a 300 x 125 mm opening through the kerb unit which is tapered to form a connection with a 100 mm pipe at the back.

Special high thick kerbs are made for the control of large vehicles on highways, but these are unlikely to be used in landscape work. They are designed to direct the wheels away from the edge of the road and to stop the vehicle from overturning should it hit the kerb, and are usually found on the outside of dangerous bends. They can be used where large vehicles must be physically prevented from crossing pedestrian areas, but it is better to achieve this by good road layout or by changes in level which form part of the landscape design. They can also be used as low retaining units for shallow planters where a massive appearance is no objection; planters in supermarket car parks are a typical situation where these units could be useful.

Natural stone kerbs to British Standard 435

Though not much used nowadays because of the high cost, natural stone is better looking and harder wearing than concrete. British Standard 435 gives the requirements for kerbs, which must be made of igneous rock such as basalt, gabbro, granite and porphyry – in practice this means whinstone or granite. Two profiles are specified in the BS – edge kerb and flat kerb, with a minimum length of 600 mm. No maximum length is given in the Standard, but as there are not many paviours capable of handling quarter tonne stones, kerbs must be made as short as possible for easy working. The sizes given in the Standard are:

edge kerb 600 mm long
200 mm wide 300 mm deep (no references are given in the Standard)
150   300
150   250
150   200
125   250
flat kerb 600 mm long
300 mm wide 200 mm deep (no references are given in the Standard)
300   150
250   125
250   150

Because working hard stones is difficult and expensive, only the top and 125 mm of the front and 75 mm of the back are dressed. Dressing may be Type A 'fine picked'; type B 'single axed' or 'nidged'; or Type C 'rough punched'. Rough punched dressing is most suitable for kerbs as the coarser texture gives better foothold and wears longer. Curved stone kerbs and the channels to match, are available made to order to the radius specified, but they are very expensive. A cheaper way of turning corners is to use one of the two standard quadrants; Type X is a segment of a circle, and Type Y is a quarter circle. Both these are made to order to the size specified by the landscape designer. The foundations, laying and bedding of natural stone kerbs are similar to those specified for precast concrete kerbs. Reused natural stone kerbs are not likely to comply with the standard sizes and profiles.

Laying and bedding kerbs

A proper foundation must be laid to support the kerbs as they will have to take considerable point and side loads from vehicles (see Figure 5.2). Even designated pedestrian areas may be subject to assault from emergency vehicles, most of which are very heavy and which may have to be driven at speed over obstacles. Before the foundation is laid, the sub-strate must be consolidated and any weak spots dug out and filled with weak concrete. Any drainage or other service trenches passing under the kerbs (and there are sure to be plenty of them) must be carefully backfilled with granular material Type 1 and rammed in 150 mm layers, though preferably not so hard that the service pipe is broken as this will cause acrimonious site disputes as well as creating bad feeling among local residents. As with all paving work, the landscape designer should make sure that all the temporary and permanent service runs are completed before the paving and kerbs are laid. The foundation to the kerbs may be either an extension to the paving sub-base itself, projecting at least 150 mm beyond the kerb, or a separate strip foundation. Separate foundations should be BS 5328 Standard Mix ST2 concrete 150 mm thick and 325 mm wide, which allows for a good thickness of haunching (the backing which supports the unit against lateral pressure) behind the units.

The kerbs are laid with the greater part of the unit below the surface so as to avoid overturning it under pressure. The minimum kerb check (the part projecting above the road surface) should be 25 mm, and the maximum for a standard 305 mm high kerb would be 125 mm. Even large traditional granite kerbs weighing a sixth of a tonne can be overset by a heavy vehicle unless properly laid, and some common failures in kerb laying are shown in Figure 5.2. Kerbs are bedded on 1:3 cement:sand mortar or 1:3 lime:sand mortar; not less than 25 mm thick for small edgings and up to 40 mm thick for large kerbs. The sand should be specified as grade M or F to BS 882. They are then haunched with BS 5328 Standard Mix ST1 concrete which should come at least two-thirds of the way up the back of the unit. Kerb bedding is shown in Figures 5.2 and 5.3.

Another method is to lay the units on a well-compacted layer of semi-dry ST2 concrete 150 mm thick and haunch them as before. In both methods, the units are finally tamped into line and level with a wooden or rubber maul, since steel hammers may damage the finish. The units may be dry-jointed with a maximum gap of 2 mm, or they may be laid with 6 mm wide joints in 1:6 cement:sand mortar, either struck flush as the work proceeds or raked out and pointed afterwards. Where the kerb is used in conjunction with a channel the joint must be filled to provide a waterproof conduit for surface water. The tolerance for variation between adjoining units is 3 mm, as it is assumed that no one can trip over a 3 mm upstand.

In long straight runs, or where the kerbs meet in situ concrete surfaces, special hot or cold jointing sealants should be used which can accommodate variations in movement; there are many different types of these on the market with complex chemical structures, and the landscape designer should get technical guidance from the manufacturer before specifying a particular type. The most usual types are flexible epoxide, 2-part polysulphide or 2-part polyurethane 10 mm thick. Where considerable movement is expected, because of unstable ground conditions, extra heavy traffic, or extreme heat and cold, the actual movement of the edge units must be calculated and the movement joint designed accordingly. This calculation is only likely to form part of the landscape designer's job when working on motorway or seaside projects, and in these circumstances a civil engineer should be available to calculate the movement joints accurately in conjunction with the main hard surfacing. Any movement joints in the paving or roadway must be

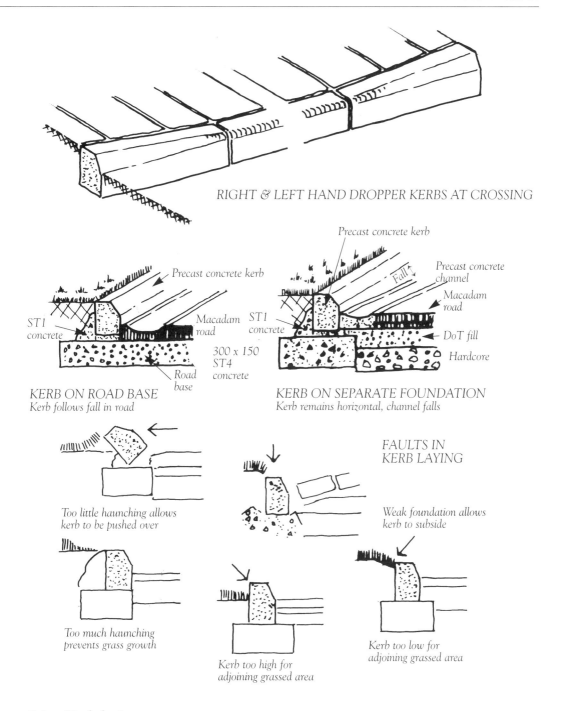

RIGHT & LEFT HAND DROPPER KERBS AT CROSSING

Precast concrete kerb

ST1 concrete

Macadam road

KERB ON ROAD BASE
Kerb follows fall in road

300 x 150 ST4 concrete

Road base

Precast concrete kerb

Fall

ST1 concrete

Precast concrete channel

Macadam road

DoT fill

Hardcore

KERB ON SEPARATE FOUNDATION
Kerb remains horizontal, channel falls

FAULTS IN KERB LAYING

Too little haunching allows kerb to be pushed over

Weak foundation allows kerb to subside

Too much haunching prevents grass growth

Kerb too high for adjoining grassed area

Kerb too low for adjoining grassed area

Figure 5.2   Kerb laying

107

continued through the kerb or edging. For kerbs dividing paving from grassed or planted areas, the 2 mm dry joint will act quite well as a movement joint, since kerbs in this situation are not likely to experience the excessive hot and cold conditions found in major roadways.

5.2 EDGINGS

British Standard edgings are also covered by BS 7263; they are very light precast concrete units designed for retention of earth in planted areas, grassed areas, or pathways where machinery or vehicles are not expected to cross the edging. While they do have to pass BS tests for transverse strength, they are not intended for heavy use. It is tempting to specify edging units as a way of forming drainage channels or mowing strips, as they are much cheaper than proper channels or kerbs, but edgings are comparatively slim in section and therefore more liable to fracture under load. They should not be considered as substitutes for the heavier units, as if they are used improperly they are a potential source of defects which can lead to injuries, claims and disputes.

They are made in three profiles to suit the type of paving or soft landscape adjoining them (see Table 5.1).

In addition to the British Standard range, most manufacturers of paving make edgings to match their slabs or blocks, usually in much the same sizes and profiles as the BS units. Among the special types available is the replica Victorian 'rope-edge' edging made of very narrow hard brick or terracotta, and there are many other profiles in brick or precast concrete including those with crenelated, wavy, curved and peaked tops. Although they have a place in conservation work and in highly ornamental landscape detailing, they are only suitable for decorative edging to planted areas where no traffic will cross them.

Brick edgings

Bricks set on edge or on end make perfectly good edgings to paving, provided that they are carefully selected and properly laid. Only engineering brick of class A or class B is really dense and weather resistant enough to stand up to the impact of light traffic and machinery and to resist frost and waterlogging. Hard dense bricks

Table 5.1 British Standard edgings		
Round top type ER (mm)	Flat top type EF (mm)	Bull-nosed top type EBN (mm)
150 x 50	150 x 50	150 x 50
200 x 50	200 x 50	200 x 50
250 x 50	250 x 50	250 x 50

such as DPC bricks of class FL or FN to BS 3921 (frost resistant) are suitable for lightly loaded areas, but the brickmaker should be informed of the proposed use before submitting samples. Double bull-nose bricks laid as headers are most suitable if the edging is to project above the paving, but square edge bricks are satisfactory if there is no risk of the arrises being chipped by mowers or other ground maintenance machinery. Brick edging to granular paving or soft landscape areas should be laid on a concrete foundation and bedded and haunched in the same way as concrete edging, but the joints will normally be 6 mm wide, filled and struck flush as the work proceeds. If the landscape designer wants to lay the bricks flat rather than on edge, then a 150 mm thick foundation of BS 5328 Standard Mix ST2 concrete projecting at least 75 mm each side of the brick, together with full bedding and jointing in 1:3 cement:sand or 1:3 sand:lime mortar should be specified. Brick edging to brick paving laid on concrete will be constructed as part of the paving. Typical details are shown in Figure 5.3.

Proprietary edge restraints

A number of manufacturers make special edging units to match their own paving. In particular, concrete block paving is often edged with small units which are a match in size and colour for the paving blocks; they are called 'edge restraints' rather than kerbs as their chief purpose is to keep the block paving in place while it is being laid, but they have the same functions as standard kerbs, though they are not as suitable for heavy loading or frequent vehicle overrun. Edge restraint units can be bull-nosed or angled, and droppers, transition kerbs and channels can be made to match the units. The construction of their foundations and the methods of bedding and jointing should be the same as those used for the block paving.

Foundations, bedding and jointing

Where precast concrete edgings are used as trim to paving laid on a concrete base, they will be laid on the same base and bedded in the same way as the paving. If they are used as trim to paving laid on a vibrated sand base, or granular paving such as gravel or hoggin, they should be laid on a proper foundation and haunched in the same way as kerbs. This also applies to edgings used to demarcate or restrain soft landscape areas. Only a comparatively small foundation is needed for these light units; BS 5328 Standard Mix ST2 concrete (using sulphate-resisting Portland cement) 150 mm wide and 100 mm deep will be adequate, but the foundation must be laid on a properly consolidated sub-strate. If the sub-strate is not stable or if the edging is placed in grassed or planted areas, the foundation should be laid on a 150 mm thick layer of well-rammed hardcore extending 75 mm each side of the foundation. Edgings are bedded in 1:3 cement:sand or 1:3 lime:sand mortar at least 25 mm thick, and the haunching is placed on the soft side of the edging (or on both sides if the paving is granular). The method of laying and the tolerances for levels are the same as those specified for kerbs. As the edgings are only 50 mm

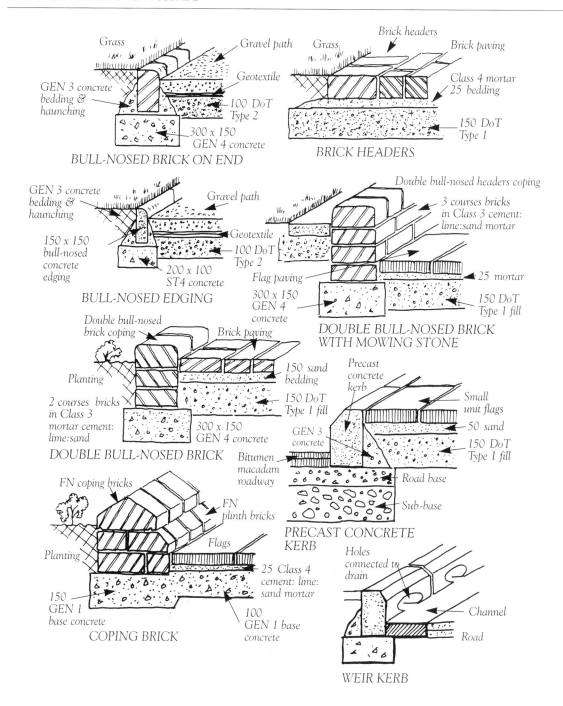

Figure 5.3   Kerbs and edgings: details

thick, it is not practicable to form satisfactory filled joints between the units, and it is better to leave a 2 mm open joint. Edgings are not normally used in conjunction with channels, so the need for forming waterproof joints does not arise. A typical bull-nosed edging to a gravel path is shown in Figure 5.3.

Junctions

Good paving design includes the design of the junctions between the paving and other landscape features. Junctions with grass, and planted areas, are usually made with kerbs or edgings of one sort or another, but junctions with walls and fences must be considered in conjunction with the wall design. Unless the architect has provided a plinth to the building (very unlikely these days) the landscape designer should arrange that the paving leads neatly up to the building and does not just crash into it. Raised brick or stone plinth courses, granite or concrete setts, and precast concrete kerbs can be used to form the junction, and any of these units will help to form a good definition for cobble paving. Small brick or sett units can be used to make up a paving module in order to avoid cutting the slabs if the wall is not parallel with the paving courses or where downpipes and other bits of building fabric intrude into the paving. Where the paving slopes in relation to the wall, one or more courses of brick ease the transition between horizontal brick courses and sloping pavement; they also form a demarcation line which stops the paving from being laid above the damp course. The edging units should either be too narrow to trip people, or so wide that they can be used as steps. Some typical junctions of paving with walls are shown in Figures 5.4 and 5.5.

Curved junctions with walls can be useful as a pedestrian deterrent, and are good for keeping trolleys and cars away from walls, but they are a very strong feature and should be used with care. Curves can be as little as 300 mm diameter or as large as the height of the wall allows. Setts, small interlocking blocks laid horizontally and cobbles will take a small curve reasonably well, while larger curves over 1 m diameter can be laid with ordinary paving bricks, blocks or pavers. Standard special radial bricks are manufactured to various radii; these can be laid either as headers or stretchers and give a very neat appearance (as shown in Figure 5.4), though it is essential to design the curve to match the available standard brick radii; designing the curve first is expensive on 'special' special bricks. The placing of seats and bollards, and the drainage of the paving are complicated by curved junctions, and should be set out on plan before the curve is designed. The ends of curves and the relationship of curved junctions to sloping paving require a lot of thought and their construction should be carefully worked out; unless the solution is straightforward curved junctions are best avoided (see Figure 5.4).

Junctions with fences are not so conspicuous, but a neat finish to the paving can be made with ordinary kerbs or edgings or by laying different paving units under the line of the fence. Circular fence posts, whether timber or steel, can be set in small squares of cobbles or setts without cutting the paving slabs; this makes it easy to replace them without dislodging the surrounding paving, as illustrated in Figure 5.5.

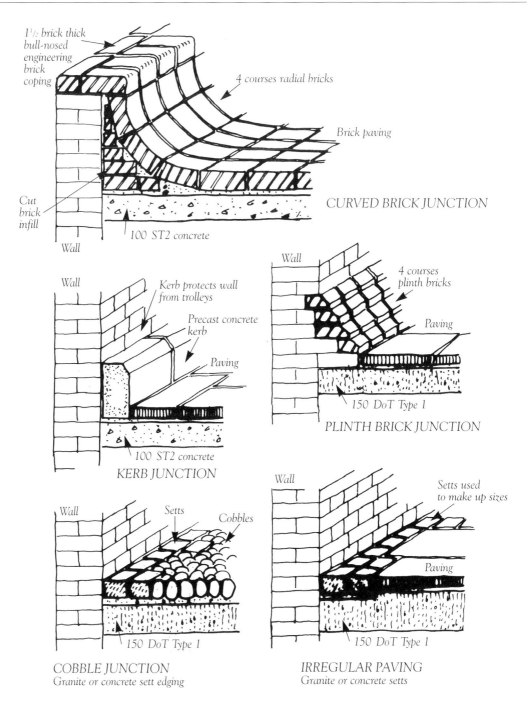

Figure 5.4 Junctions with walls

Wire fencing, metal railings and steel fence posts can all drip rust, acid rain, or paint on to paving and an edging of dark units can disguise this unsightly staining.

Junctions can be made with raised edgings or kerbs to direct water away from a wall, or by means of channels to guide the run-off to a gully. Raised junctions also act as protection to the fence or wall against mowers, trolleys, prams or wheelbarrows. Spur stones are often used to protect corners of walls and piers against traffic, but unless they form part of the wall construction they can trap dirt and rubbish, while a raised junction will do the same job without creating awkward corners.

5.3 MOWING STONES

This is the traditional term for the narrow flat strip of hard paving laid along the base of a wall, high kerb, or step to prevent the scythe from hitting the wall when cutting grass close to it. Not only did such an impact mean a visit to the smith to repair the blade, but the scytheman's arms would have been badly jarred, and the carelessness would cost him a few pints for his jeering fellow workmen. The modern motor mower may not feel the impact as much, but the damage to blades or casing may be equally expensive. A mowing stone also reduces the amount of strimmer cord expended on slashing the wall.

Another original function of the mowing stone was to catch the drip from the gutterless eaves of the building and to direct it away from the wall – not so necessary now when gutters are fitted to nearly all buildings, but still a useful protection for garden walls liable to frost attack. A further benefit is the protection of the wall from rising damp; while all well-built garden walls have damp-proof courses it is only too easy for the soil to be worked up above the DPC, and the provision of a firmly bedded mowing stone will help to prevent this from happening. If the hard strip is continued along planted areas adjoining the wall, it will also prevent plants from being placed too close to the wall and reduce the amount of mud staining from splashes. A mowing stone at the foot of a wall next to a roadway or car park will also help to keep bitumen macadam or gravel from marking the brickwork, and will provide a straight clean finish to the soft material. Visually the mowing stone makes a pleasant transition between wall and ground.

Nowadays the mowing stone is usually a precast concrete channel or brick on edge strip 150 to 225 mm wide, but cobbles, setts, old kerbs laid flat, or broken flags trimmed to size can be used. Dished concrete or brick channels can be used to provide surface drainage at the same time if this is necessary. The strip should be laid 25 mm below the finished surface of grassed areas and laid to slope away from the wall. Mowing stones in soft landscape are usually bedded in 1:6 lime:sand mortar laid on a 150 mm layer of well-rammed hardcore; where the mowing stone is continued across an access route the units should be set on a concrete foundation to prevent subsidence. Mowing stones at the edge of granular or bitumen paving should be laid on the same base as the paving itself.

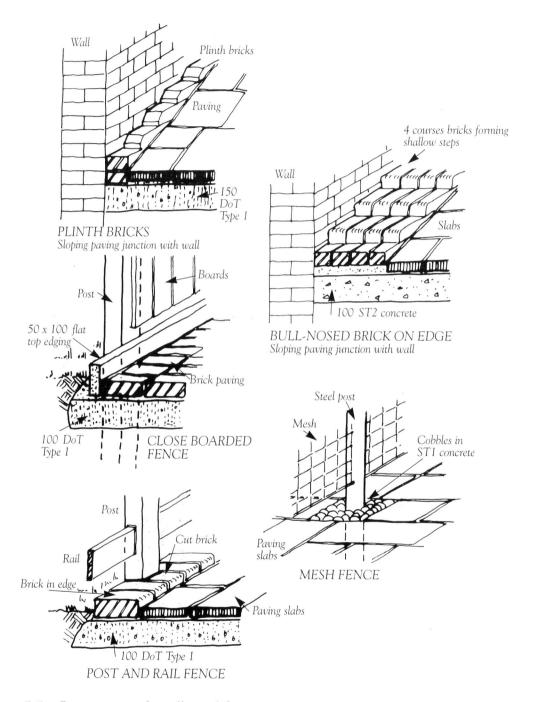

Figure 5.5   Junctions with walls and fences

5.4 TREE GRILLES

Tree grilles are the open sections of paving laid around trees in solid paving in order to allow rainwater to percolate through to the tree roots. Tree grilles can be made from the same material as the main paving, or they can be made of a contrasting material. Tree grilles can be either pre-formed or constructed in situ. Pre-formed grilles can be made of precast concrete, cast iron, hardwood, or (for the very rich) bronze. In-situ grilles can be made from small paving units such as bricks, pavers, concrete or granite setts, cobbles, grass concrete blocks or pedestrian deterrent paving. Nearly all manufacturers provide paving support frames which are inserted under the surrounding paving so that all the units settle together, and which can be filled with the paving material. The slots in the frames allow water to penetrate to the tree roots. These frames are remarkably vandal-proof and have the advantage of displaying a continuous surface, though the slots do not allow so much water through as open grilles. Alternatively, there is a good case for planting trees in slightly raised planters as long as the watering problem can be solved. The size of tree grille and the tree hole in the centre must be chosen foremost with regard to the tree; the eventual girth of the trunk will determine the size of the hole, and the water needs of the tree together with the amount of available surface water will determine the size of the grille. Some types are supplied with inner grilles for use while the tree is small, which are removed as the tree grows, but unless the ground staff can be trusted to remove them as necessary, they can cause severe damage by constricting the bole.

There are a number of points to consider when selecting tree grilles:

- Unfixed grilles can be picked up by vandals and destroyed or used as weapons, but fixed grilles must be removable for maintenance; a special key can be provided for this purpose.
- Grilles must allow for the tree to expand its trunk to the full size.
- Litter should not be trapped in grille openings.
- The filling to the grille openings should allow water to pass through freely, as in large hard surfaced areas there is no rainfall available except that which passes through the grille. It is therefore desirable to design the paving to fall towards the grille, but not if the area is full of parked cars dripping petrol and oil. In this case the paving should fall away from the grille, and the tree may need regular watering. Valuable trees can be supplied with water by land drains laid to conduct water to their roots, but this method needs careful design.
- Very few grilles can stand heavy vehicles, so some form of barrier is needed to keep them away from the grille (and also away from the tree).
- Grilles must allow for tree guards and stakes to be fixed.
- Weed control is a problem, and the client must be told that regular maintenance will be required. Total herbicides are not very good for the tree.

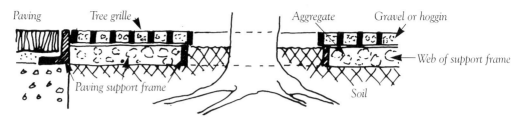

TYPICAL CAST OR DUCTILE IRON TREE GRILLE ON PAVING SUPPORT FRAME

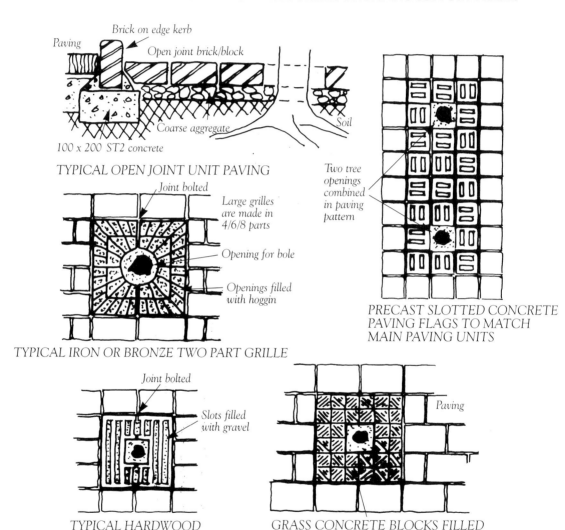

TYPICAL OPEN JOINT UNIT PAVING

TYPICAL IRON OR BRONZE TWO PART GRILLE

PRECAST SLOTTED CONCRETE
PAVING FLAGS TO MATCH
MAIN PAVING UNITS

TYPICAL HARDWOOD
TWO PART GRILLE

GRASS CONCRETE BLOCKS FILLED
WITH GRAVEL OR HOGGIN

Figure 5.6   Tree grilles

- As settlement of the soil is inevitable, the grille must rest directly on the soil and move with the soil (thereby creating tripping edges) or be supported by a grille support frame. If the grille rests on the adjoining paving only, even light loads will be liable to fracture it.

Precast concrete grilles

These are usually designed by manufacturers to fit in with their own special modular paving units, being consistent in size and finish; they are made in multiples of the ordinary paving flag, with a smaller or larger number of perforations according to the amount of water to be allowed through. Some patterns have round or square holes, some have slots and some have recessed edges – the choice is a matter of visual effect. Concrete grilles are usually heavy enough not to be readily lifted by vandals and those types which have interlocking nibs are less likely to settle unevenly as the tree takes up the soil nutrients. A group of pre-cast concrete grilles is shown in Figure 5.6.

Cast iron grilles

These are more elegant and expensive than concrete, since much finer sections and more complicated patterns are possible. Cast iron is a brittle material, and therefore support frames should be used where the grilles must be level with the adjoining paving. The construction of this type of grille is shown in Figure 5.6. Ductile iron, which is less brittle than cast iron is coming into more common use, and the landscape designer should use this material in preference. Grilles are made in a wide range of sizes and patterns, circular, square, rectangular or oval; the larger sizes are made in two, four or six sections for easy handling. Since they are expensive, cast iron grilles tend to be used in expensive paving, and they look particularly well in brick or natural stone paving. A square two-part grille is illustrated in Figure 5.6. Typical sizes available are:

- with 300 mm diameter hole: square 456 x 456, 606 x 606, 1000 x 1000 mm;
- with 600 mm diameter hole: circular 800, 1000, 1200 and 1400 mm diameter;
- with 600 x 600 mm hole: square 800 x 800, 1000 x 1000, 1200 x 1200, 1400 x 1400 and 1500 x 1500 mm;
- with 800 x 800 mm hole: square 1800 x 1800 mm.

Hardwood grilles

These should be teak or iroko, and are really only satisfactory on sheltered ground or for interior planting such as shopping malls. A typical hardwood grille is shown in Figure 5.6. The conscientious landscape designer will, of course, specify that the timber must come from ecologically sound sources. They are expensive and they have rather a nautical look reminiscent of teak yacht gratings which may or may

117

Plate 20   *Traditional cast iron tree grille with gravel fill. These grilles have sunk slightly below the paving, some of them very unevenly. There is no provision for enlarging the tree hole when the tree is fully grown.*

not suit the landscape designer's plan. If they are used on raised planters they can double up very well as seats or tables, and for this purpose they are better than concrete or cast iron grilles which are chilly to sit on except in the warmest weather. For interior landscapes such as shopping malls and atria the fill below them should be capable of supporting the weight of a large shopper or two, and for this purpose big cobbles or broken stone do very well. Litter trapping is also a problem with a loose fill; the grilles should be removable with a key.

In-situ grilles

These are usually made of the units used for the paving, and are formed by leaving open joints in the regular pattern, or by laying a special pattern with wide dry joints, as shown in Figure 5.6. The snag with these small units is that if they are set in concrete to prevent vandalism, they do not allow enough water through, while if they are laid loose they can be easily lifted and hurled at the nearest plate glass window. Protected grounds and private gardens are the safest places for small unit grilles. The problem with this method is that the grille units will look unsightly if

Plate 21 *A hardwood tree grille which looks well in the setting, although the spillage of gravel from the tree pit rather spoils the effect.*

they settle unevenly into the tree pit, and the best way to overcome this is to lay an edging or kerb flush with the paving to demarcate the grille area so that settlement is controlled. In-situ grilles allow the landscape designer to create irregular shapes such as trefoils, diamonds, serpentines, or to link several tree pits in a single grille. Brick pavers, or the perforated hard bricks used for damp courses, natural stone slabs, setts, small concrete flags, and grass concrete with large openings filled with gravel or hoggin – but not cobbles or shingle – are all suitable materials for in-situ grilles (see Figure 5.6). Short clayware or concrete agricultural drain pipes of 100 or 150 mm diameter set on end and filled with coarse gravel provide plenty of access area for water if the circle pattern is acceptable within the overall paving design; this method is particularly useful for trees with high water needs. Loose gravel or aggregate is sometimes used for covering tree pits in lieu of grilles, but this is only suitable for private gardens where reliable gardeners can be trusted not to sweep it all out.

Bases and bedding

Obviously no sub-base is required for tree grilles, but the soil around the tree must be capable of supporting the grille at about the same level as the adjoining paving, unless of course the grille is deliberately designed to be at a different level or if a grille support frame is used. The grille should be laid on a 50 or 75 mm layer of neutral aggregate (just a little larger than the openings in the grille) over an open textured soil; this aggregate also helps to discourage weeds. Topping up with more aggregate may be necessary as the soil sinks. Fine pea gravel looks well, but tends to get swept out of the grille during normal street cleaning operations or heavy rain, while bark or woodchips can be burnt, and will eventually decompose to provide a good meal for weeds and fungi.

Amsterdam Tree Soil planting

There is a technique for planting trees in urban sites known as the Amsterdam Tree Soil method; this involves planting the tree in a large shallow tree pit in a special soil which is combined with nutrients. This special soil can be consolidated in layers in the same way as DoT Granular Fill so that it is capable of supporting the paving equally well without damaging the tree roots. Consequently, the paving and the tree grille both settle at the same rate, thus obviating any risk of damage from uneven settlement.

6   DRAINAGE OF PAVED AREAS

Paving of all kinds must be drained. A paved area which is not properly drained is not only unsightly but hazardous to users as it will accumulate standing pools of water; it will grow moss, algae or other undesirable vegetation; it can also develop stains from the chemicals contained in run-off water. Even if the paving units themselves are frost resistant, in winter there will be a further hazard of icy patches, particularly dangerous for the elderly and disabled. Frozen water in the joints may lead to spalling surfaces and frost-heave. It is only too easy to think of paving as being a flat carpet laid on the ground, but the falls needed for good drainage result in a much bigger change in levels than is usually appreciated. The correct placing of drainage outlets will also help to make the paving safer and more comfortable to walk on; there cannot be any landscape designer who has not got wet feet trying to dodge a blocked drain outlet set unavoidably in the centre of the path. All the unpleasant effects of waterlogging can be avoided by proper drainage. There are two design factors to be considered; the falls and channels of the paving itself, and the drains which carry the water to its disposal point.

Whilst the drawings of a building surrounded by paving may show the surface as a neat horizontal line on the elevations, the need to provide drainage falls makes this impractical. If the landscape designer is responsible for the external paving, it is advisable to discuss with the architect the predicted usage of these areas, as the manner in which falls in long runs of paving are made will be governed by this. The use of extra steps and ramping to entrances must be considered in detail, and the final details are best left until the finished floor level of the entrance is fixed on site, as it is not uncommon to see buildings with a 'squint' or half step at the entrances which obviously have not had their levels coordinated. In classical architecture, the base of the building was embellished with plinths or base courses, against which the fall of the paving could be gracefully arranged, but where a modern building is designed with the brickwork thumping straight into the ground, the landscape designer may have to allow for a kerb, mowing strip, or edging to take up the falls.

It is very important to give the client an accurate plan of the drainage runs as laid (not as shown on original drawings), since the actual site layout can vary considerably from the landscape designer's intentions, and the workers who carry out work on the site at a later date will not usually appreciate the importance of surface water drainage systems.

6.1 CHANNELS

Channels carry surface water to a drainage outlet and there are numerous ways of achieving a good relationship between the channel and the paving; by laying different coloured or textured units along the drain line, by laying completely different units such as lines of bricks in concrete paving slabs, by laying units in different directions so as to meet at a drainage line, or by using purpose made drainage channels. Grass concrete, gravel and hoggin are self-draining.

Pre-formed channels are flat or dished rectangular units of stone or precast concrete, or small units which are used to form a smooth evenly graded conduit for surface water. They may be used adjoining a kerb or edging, or on their own in the centre or sides of a paved area. When the drainage layout for the site is the dominant factor determining the levels for paving and channels it is essential to lay a correctly graded channel first and then to dress the road or pathway material to that profile. Examples of these may be seen in Figure 6.1. The channel will normally discharge into drainage gulleys at regular intervals, though where open ground adjoins the road or pathway it may be permissible to discharge the surface water directly into a ditch. Three factors control the gradient of channels and the spacing of gulleys:

- the need to keep any adjoining kerb check at a reasonable height;
- the need to keep the channel at a good fall;
- the amount of run-off to be carried.

Although steeper slopes can theoretically drain more water, a channel can only carry a certain amount of water without overflowing, and it is therefore sensible to keep the gulleys at the normal spacing regardless of the ground slope. Channels also make a good mowing strip around vertical structures, provided that Building Regulations with regard to the proximity of drains to buildings are met, and the channel units can double as edgings to lightly used grassed areas or paths. These only work as drainage channels where clippings are boxed off, as mats of clippings must not be allowed to obstruct the channel or block the gulleys.

Precast concrete channels

British Standard 7263 gives the sizes and profiles of precast concrete channels. Two types are available; rectangular with a flat upper surface, or rectangular with a

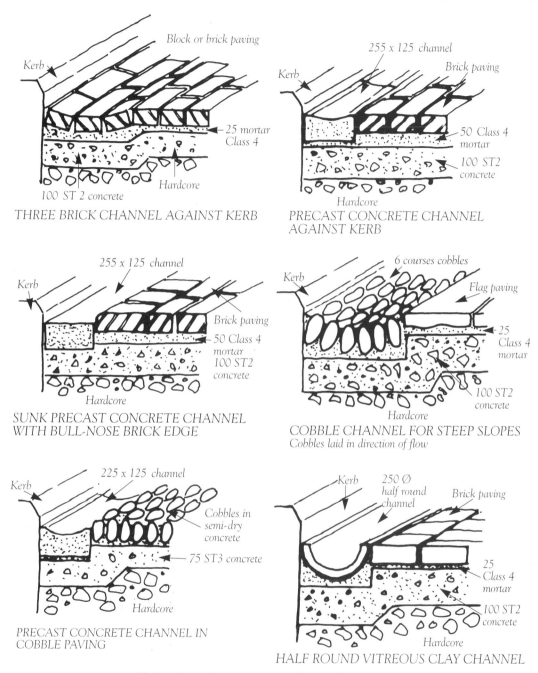

Block or brick paving

Kerb

25 mortar Class 4

Hardcore

100 ST 2 concrete

THREE BRICK CHANNEL AGAINST KERB

255 x 125 channel

Brick paving

Kerb

50 Class 4 mortar

100 ST2 concrete

Hardcore

PRECAST CONCRETE CHANNEL
AGAINST KERB

255 x 125 channel

Kerb

Brick paving

50 Class 4 mortar
100 ST2 concrete

Hardcore

SUNK PRECAST CONCRETE CHANNEL
WITH BULL-NOSE BRICK EDGE

6 courses cobbles

Flag paving

Kerb

25 Class 4 mortar

100 ST2 concrete

Hardcore

COBBLE CHANNEL FOR STEEP SLOPES
Cobbles laid in direction of flow

225 x 125 channel

Kerb

Cobbles in semi-dry concrete

75 ST3 concrete

Hardcore

PRECAST CONCRETE CHANNEL IN
COBBLE PAVING

Kerb 250 Ø half round channel

Brick paving

25 Class 4 mortar

100 ST2 concrete

Hardcore

HALF ROUND VITREOUS CLAY CHANNEL

All channel units laid in 1:1:6 cement:lime:sand mortar

Figure 6.1   Channels

123

25 mm deep dishing which is more satisfactory on very shallow slopes or flat ground (see Figure 6.1). The dished type also allows the edge of the channel to be set flush with the adjoining paving, whereas flat channels must be set below the paving thus creating tripping ledges. Both are made in the same lengths as kerbs.

channel square 125 x 255 mm BS 7263 Type CS1
channel square 125 x 150 mm BS 7263 Type CS2
channel dished 125 x 255 mm BS 7263 Type CD

Curved channels are made to the same radii as curved kerbs, and being symmetrical they can be used for both internal and external profiles. If the channel is butted up against the kerb, it is essential to remember that the radius of an inside kerb must match the outside radius of the channel fitted to it. Conversely, the radius of an outside kerb must match the radius of the inside channel. If this seems too confusing, it is safer to specify only that kerbs and channels must match, and not to specify reference codes.

Natural stone channels

Far too expensive for ordinary landscape work, but they can be used where cost is no object. York stone can be used in conjunction with York stone paving, but where the stone channel is set in brick or a different natural stone paving, second-hand re-faced granite or whinstone setts and kerbs make good substantial channels. The method of laying and bedding is the same as for concrete channels.

Brick channels

Brick channels may be one brick wide for small paved areas, but two brick wide channels look better in wide areas. A one brick wide channel with two stretchers side by side may be sloped slightly to the centre, while a two brick wide channel of four headers may be shaped in a gentle curve from side to side. The bricks should be well burnt hard bricks, smooth and dense, preferably engineering or special quality bricks which are frost and slip-resistant. The bricks are laid lengthways as stretchers along the channel to offer the least resistance to the flow, and they should be very carefully bedded and jointed in 1:1:6 cement:lime:sand mortar. The channel should have the same foundation as the paving, but extra care must be taken to keep the falls accurate. Brick channels are mostly used in brick paving, but they are also suitable for flag paving, concrete block paving, and cobble paving where the landscape designer wishes to emphasize the line of the channel (see Figure 6.1). It is important to ensure that the paving units adjoining the channel are well fitted, especially where they have to be cut, as in the case of herring-bone brick or block paving. If possible, paving units should be laid square on to the channel and cut units kept to the edge of the paved area where irregularities are not so likely to trap water or pedestrians. Some manufacturers make dished bricks,

Plate 22 *Reclaimed granite setts, kerb and channel at the Tower of London. Materials supplied by Civil Engineering Developments, Specialists in Natural Stone. (Photograph by courtesy of Civil Engineering Developments Ltd.)*

mostly for use with their own brick paving, which may be in matching or contrasting colours.

Granite or concrete setts

Granite or concrete setts can be used to form channels, and their construction is similar to that of brick channels. These smaller units can be more attractive than brick, and are well suited to conservation work. Cobbles are sometimes used for channels, but unless they are laid low enough to allow the water to run freely (in which case they do not show much) they are only a litter trap. Cobbles do have an advantage on steep slopes in that they retard the flow of water to some extent, so preventing a rush of water down the slope.

Patent channels

There are a number of precast concrete channel systems available to the landscape designer which consist of an enclosed channel covered with a perforated concrete or steel grid; they are usually made in short lengths with a regular increment of depth in each length so that the fall is accurately controlled. Gulleys, silt traps, rodding eyes, junctions and other normal drain fittings form part of the system (see Figure 6.2). The object of these systems is to provide an accurate fall while providing a level surface for traffic in hard paved areas. This is particularly important for the drainage of aircraft aprons, ambulance entrances, fork lift trucking areas, and wheelchair access paths, where tipping or tilting of the vehicle could have unfortunate results. The grid forms a level smooth surface for wheels, and prevents debris from clogging the drain, and they are made to carry wheel loads up to 600 kN, though 50–60 kN is sufficient for pedestrian traffic. However, as the grid hides the channel, it is possible for quite a lot of fine detritus to accumulate before the maintenance staff get round to clearing it, and the grid itself can easily become choked. A typical system run would have an invert depth falling from 100 to 300 mm giving a fall of 6 per cent (1:16). The maximum length of a run before discharge is about 30 m. These systems can also be had with level inverts if required for laying in sloping ground.

Although the laying and bedding of patent drain systems follows much the same

Plate 23 *Gridded channels are excellent if they are kept clean; this one shows the result of a lack of maintenance by the owner, British Rail.*

principles as ordinary concrete drains, the manufacturer should be required to provide advice on the use of the product.

Foundations, bedding and jointing

The foundations for channels associated with kerbs will be either an extension of the roadway sub-base, or part of the kerb foundation, and the same mixes and methods of laying, bedding and jointing should be specified as for kerbs, while the movement joints should coincide with those in the kerbs. Where channels are used separately to drain a paved area, they are laid on the same base and jointed in the same way as the paving in order to keep the movement and settlement of the channels in conformation with the paving units.

Manhole and access covers

All landscape designers have suffered from seeing their beautifully designed paving marred by intrusive manhole covers thrust into the paving regardless of the pattern or material. It is important to discuss the paving design at an early stage (if at all possible) with every service engineer who has access covers in the paving so that they may be coordinated into the total design. Services which will generate manholes and access fittings of one sort or another are:

- surface water drain runs – the landscape designer has some direct control over these;
- foul drains which are the responsibility of the architect or an engineer;
- main sewers may need new manholes on the site which are the responsibility of the local authority;
- rainwater drains from buildings which are the responsibility of the architect;
- electrical cables which are the responsibility of the services engineer and the electricity board;
- gas mains and service runs which are the responsibility of the services engineer and the gas board;
- water mains and service runs which are the responsibility of the services engineer and the water board;
- telephone cables which are the responsibility of the services engineer and the telephone company or British Telecom;
- various cable companies – television, land lines, alarm systems which are the responsibility of the companies concerned;
- on large contracts there may be other service runs such as irrigation lines, fire-fighting mains, and special cable runs which should be checked;
- large main grid sewers, national gas or oil pipelines may run through the site; these have legal immunity from the landscape designer's control.

Admittedly, many of these services only need small access fittings, but they should be considered as part of the paving design, otherwise they will be spotted over the

127

surface like a bad case of measles, particularly where they have prominent markers. If possible, a number of access points should be grouped together in one area so that the visual intrusion is minimized (see Figure 6.2).

Small access points are best set in a panel of material let into the paving, as they are often circular or of a shape incompatible with the paving pattern. The panel can be made of a material matching or complementary to the paving on the same principle as the manhole covers; an arrangement of manhole covers and access point panels in the same material gives a coherence to the whole paving surface. If there are also tree grilles in the area it may be possible to use the same materials for them in order to give continuity. The three most common ways of dealing with manhole covers are: to cut the paving units round the cover; to fit the cover into an area of small unit paving which fits the paving module, or to cut the paving both inside the block cover and round it so that the paving appears continuous. This last method requires the services of an expert angle-grinder user; it is therefore expensive, noisy and very dusty indeed, and it is probably only worth using on prestige jobs.

Plate 24 *Well integrated manhole covers showing how careful block filling can reduce the impact of angled manholes in paving. Wakefield Cathedral precinct paving design by Tess Jaray. (Photograph by courtesy of Terry Knight Consultancy.)*

Plate 25 *A well-cast manhole cover with clear name, date and BS reference, though badly laid in the adjoining granite setts. Early manhole covers were cast with ornamental patterns, and modern ones could be equally attractive.*

The most conspicuous intruders are the drain manhole covers. In order to reduce their impact they should be set parallel with the paving pattern if possible; if not (and it is unusual to find manholes exactly parallel) a wide enough margin should be left round the manhole for coordinating material to be fitted easily. The cover itself should be designed to harmonize with the paving. Most manufacturers now make 'block' cover frames which can be filled with any material; the landscape designer can either choose a material complementary to the paving or units which match the paving (see Figure 6.2). For example:

- brick paving and matching brick cover fill;
- precast concrete flags and textured concrete cover fill;
- granite setts and complementary exposed aggregate concrete fill;
- York stone paving and ornamental cast iron cover;
- grass concrete blocks and textured concrete fill;
- plain or interlocking concrete blocks and matching block fill;
- gravel or hoggin and exposed aggregate cover fill.

129

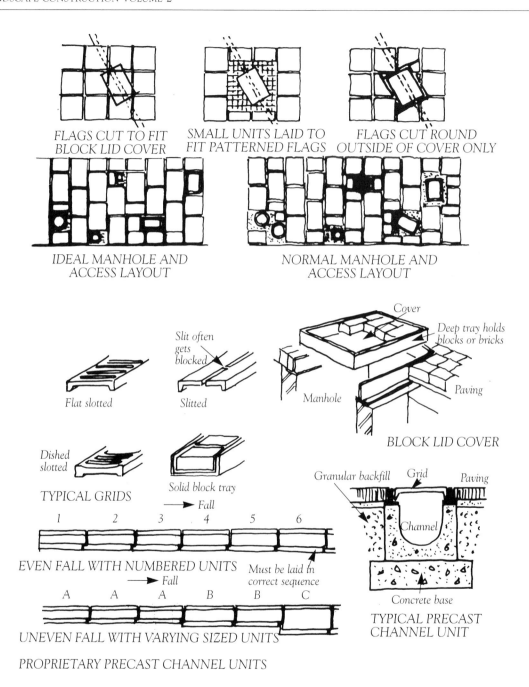

FLAGS CUT TO FIT
BLOCK LID COVER

SMALL UNITS LAID TO
FIT PATTERNED FLAGS

FLAGS CUT ROUND
OUTSIDE OF COVER ONLY

IDEAL MANHOLE AND
ACCESS LAYOUT

NORMAL MANHOLE AND
ACCESS LAYOUT

Slit often
gets
blocked

Cover

Deep tray holds
blocks or bricks

Flat slotted

Slitted

Manhole

Paving

BLOCK LID COVER

Dished
slotted

Solid block tray

Granular backfill   Grid   Paving

Channel

TYPICAL GRIDS

Fall

Concrete base

1   2   3   4   5   6

TYPICAL PRECAST
CHANNEL UNIT

EVEN FALL WITH NUMBERED UNITS   Must be laid in
correct sequence

Fall

A   A   A   B   B   C

UNEVEN FALL WITH VARYING SIZED UNITS

PROPRIETARY PRECAST CHANNEL UNITS

Figure 6.2   Manholes and gridded drains

130

6.2 SURFACE WATER DRAINAGE

Design of drainage falls and channels for paved areas

The term 'fall' means the drop in level from the highest part of a section of paved area to the channel which carries away the water. The 'channel' is the open conduit which directs the water to a gulley. The 'gulley' is the opening into the drain pipe which carries the collected water away to its final destination, which can be a sewer, soakaway, stream, pond or lake. The 'camber' is the gentle curve across a path or road which directs water to both sides of the path, while the term 'cross-fall' is used where the water is directed to one side only.

The falls recommended by various advisory organizations are adequate for small paved areas where there is not likely to be a large accumulation of water, but in open spaces more generous falls are required for the following reasons:

- In open spaces where the wind can have free play, water may be driven up against the falls, and will not clear easily unless the falls are adequate.
- The accumulation of leaves or litter may lie across the paving in drifts; extra falls are needed to allow water to pass the obstructions.
- Paving in small areas is often more carefully constructed than paving in large areas, and is more likely to be laid on a homogeneous base, whereas a large area may be laid on several different sub-strates with a greater probability of uneven subsidence which will result in ponding. Wherever possible, changes in the level of the paving should coincide with changes in the sub-strate.

Channels should not run across the route of pedestrians; if they must do so, the crossing should be at the highest end of the channel where there is least water and the channel is shallowest. Also if the drainage layout permits, the gulleys which collect the surface water into the drain pipe should be placed where ponding will not obstruct pedestrians or vehicles, as they will inevitably get blocked by leaves, litter and other detritus (however well they may be maintained) with the result that the trapped water can be splashed on to people or buildings (see Figure 6.3).

To comply with Building Regulations, all external surfaces, including paving, must be at least 150 mm below the damp course of the building. The paving should be laid to fall away from buildings, as otherwise any ponding caused by blocked gulleys might rise above the damp course, and if the water is allowed to stand for some time, staining and algal growth on the brick or stone work could develop, and in severe cases, the building structure itself could become wet, leading to expensive remedial work and compensation. If the ground is so contoured that a slope towards buildings is unavoidable, there are several ways of dealing with the problem, such as:

- laying a channel about 500 mm away from the building large enough to take all run-off;

- providing a glacis (or steep slope) at the foot of the building so that water is thrown back on to the paving.

There will be occasions where basement or semi-basement rooms adjoin paved areas, and more stringent precautions against flooding are needed. The traditional (and expensive) solution is to construct a 'dry area' adjoining the building. This consists of a trench with a retaining wall supporting the paving and a clear space between it and the building wide enough to allow for maintenance; the bottom of the trench is below the lowest floor level, and is paved and drained (see Figure 6.3). This trench must be protected from pedestrians and vehicles by a protective barrier complying with BS 6180 and the Building Regulations. Obviously this is only possible where drainage can be obtained at a level below the basement, and if this cannot be done the alternative is to construct a deep drain channel about 500 mm from the building protected by gratings so that it cannot be easily blocked, and discharging into an over-sized drain pipe to avoid any risk of flooding.

Where paved areas abut planted areas, the landscape designer will have to use his or her judgement whether or not to allow water to drain on to the earth; this will depend on the amount of water running off the paving, the thirstiness of the plants and the presence of chemicals inimical to plants on the paving. This sort of problem occurs in car and lorry parks with planted areas where oil and petrol seepage may take place, and if in doubt the landscape designer should avoid run-off on to planted areas, either by using raised planters or by ensuring a positive fall to the paving away from plants. In general, run-off should not be allowed on to grassed areas, as this may cause slippery patches, besides waterlogging the grass roots and bogging down machinery. However, where the paving is pedestrian only, and the adjoining grass is only for ornamental or amenity purposes, French drains laid at the junction of grass and paving can be used to carry run-off to the drainage system; either plain gravel filled drains or the more elaborate type with vertical fin drains are suitable; these are described in Section 6.3, Land Drainage.

Calculation of paving drainage

The principal guidance for drainage design is contained in BS 6367 *Drainage of Roofs and Paved Areas*. This British Standard gives recommendations for various weather conditions, rates of water flow, and recommended falls for a range of circumstances.

The amount of water falling on a paved area varies with its location in the British Isles; the northern parts have more rain, but it is evenly distributed throughout the year, whilst the southern parts have less rain but with more sudden heavy outbursts. It is advisable to allow for the occasional heavy rainfall rather than for the regular small rainfall, as it is the heavy rainfall (even of short duration) that can overflow drainage systems and cause havoc with expensive basement installations, traffic and underground services. The BS gives five 'design rates' for such heavy rainfall; 50 mm per hour, 75 mm per hour, 100 mm per hour, 150 mm

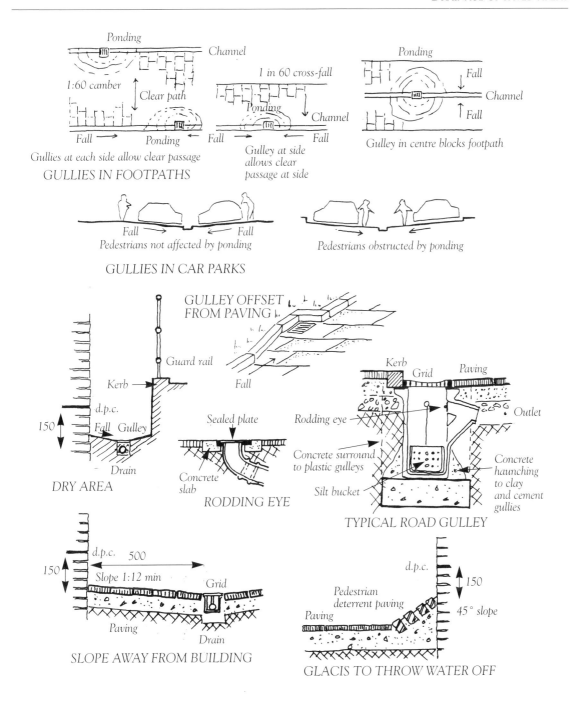

Figure 6.3   Surface water drainage

per hour and 225 mm per hour. These 'design rates' represent the maximum rate of run-off in a two minute period. The landscape designer should determine the design rate to be adopted; in most cases this will be the lowest level given in the BS – that is, 50 mm per hour – resulting in temporary ponding after the rain has ceased, but where ponding cannot be accepted (such as ambulance entrances and areas frequented by disabled people, or shopping malls) a level of 75 mm per hour should be used in the design calculations. The higher values are mostly used for flat roof design where excess water is completely unacceptable, while the highest rate is only applicable to conditions where installations below ground must never in any circumstances be flooded or when materials in storage are of a hazardous or irreplaceable nature. Another factor is the frequency with which these five design rates of heavy rainfall can be expected; the BS gives maps showing the frequency for all parts of the British Isles. It is interesting to note that rates of 75 mm per hour can be expected every year in southeast England, but only every 100 years in northern Scotland, though freak weather can bring several occurrences together in one year. (The BS gives figures for some frequencies of 35,000 years, but this need not cause too much worry to the landscape designer.) The actual amounts of rainwater falling on a flat surface that can be expected for each design rate are shown in Table 6.1. Naturally most of this water will drain away as fast as it falls, so that unless all the outlets are blocked it is unlikely that the depth of water shown will actually occur.

When considering the amount of rainfall, remember that sloping hard surfaces such as embankments which discharge on to the paved area will increase the amount of water that has to be drained. Vertical walls do not contribute greatly to the water flow, and they only need to be considered if even temporary ponding cannot be allowed. Strong winds can blow extra water off adjoining roofs and balconies, but if the wind and rain are that strong, most pedestrians will be looking for shelter rather than for a landscape designer to blame.

For small paved areas, one direction of fall to a channel or gulley is probably adequate, but large areas such as car parks are usually laid out with falls and cross-falls to provide better control of the water flowing over the surface. The direction

Table 6.1
Amount of rainwater falling on a flat surface

Design rate (mm per hour)	Duration in minutes, with resulting depth of water (mm)					
	1	2	3	4	5	10
50	0.83	1.67	2.50	3.33	4.17	8.33
75	1.25	2.50	3.75	5.00	6.25	12.50
100	1.67	3.33	5.00	6.67	8.33	16.67
150	2.50	5.00	7.50	10.50	12.50	25.50
225	3.75	7.50	11.25	15.00	18.75	37.50

of the falls and the spacing of channels will depend on the use of the area; for example, a car park with a gangway between two rows of cars is preferably drained away from the gangway where people walk, while a pedestrian walkway is best drained to each side, and a courtyard inside a building is best drained to the centre to provide maximum protection to the walls. Examples of these are shown in Figure 6.3. The permissible gradients for paving are the main factor controlling the spacing of channels, and the gradients recommended in the British Standard are chosen to give the best run-off compatible with safe walking or driving:

- paved areas for parking or courtyards: minimum fall is 1 in 60;
- footpaths or walkways: maximum fall is 1 in 30, minimum is 1 in 40;
- access or estate roads: maximum longitudinal fall 1 in 15; minimum cross-fall 1 in 40.

Using the normal rainfall design rate of 50 mm per hour, the rule-of-thumb for calculating the discharge from a paved area is:

$$R = A \times I \times 0.0139$$

where R is run-off in litres per second, A is the area to be drained in m^2, I is the impermeability factor, and 0.0139 is a constant conversion factor for 50 mm per hour. (0.0139 = 50 mm per hour expressed as litres per second; 0.0208 = 75 mm per hour expressed as litres per second.)

The impermeability factor depends on the impermeability of the paving unit itself, the method of bedding and the width and density of the joints. Some typical impermeability factors are:

- solid concrete or asphalt = 0.85 to 0.95 depending on density;
- mortar bedded paving flags with mortar joints = 0.75 to 0.85;
- sand bedded paving units with open joints = 0.5 to 0.7;
- paving blocks with open joints = 0.4 to 0.5;
- macadam = 0.25 to 0.6 depending on number of coats and density of material;
- gravel or hoggin = 0.15 to 0.3 depending on thickness and consolidation;
- grass = 0.05 to 0.25 depending on density of soil.

For example, an area 20 m × 20 m of sandbedded plain blocks would have a run-off of 400 m² × 0.65 × 0.0139 = 3.61 litres per second.

The surface water drainage pipes which take the discharge must be adequate for all expected flows of water, and the flow of water which can be carried by various sizes of pipe can be selected from Tables 6.2 and 6.3.

The figures given in Tables 6.2 and 6.3 are for simple projects only, and where very large or irregular flows are expected, the services of a drainage engineer should be engaged. Small bore pipes with a low flow cannot be laid at a shallow gradient, as the velocity of the water is insufficient to clean out the pipe. It is

Table 6.2
Flow of water carried by clay or concrete pipes

Gradient	1:10	1:20	1:30	1:40	1:50	1:60	1:80	1:100
Size of pipe:	Flow in litres per second:							
DN 100	15.0	8.5	6.8	5.8	5.2	4.7	4.0	3.5
DN 150	28.0	19.0	16.0	14.0	12.0	11.0	9.1	8.0
DN 225	140.0	95.0	76.0	66.0	58.0	53.0	46.0	40.0

Note: DN sizes are convenient round figures expressing the internal diameter of the pipe without taking note of manufacturer's variations.

Table 6.3
Flow of water carried by plastic pipes

Gradient	1:10	1:20	1:30	1:40	1:50	1:60	1:80	1:100
Size of pipe:	Flow in litres per second:							
82.4 mm i/dia	12.0	8.5	6.8	5.8	5.2	4.7	4.0	3.5
110 mm i/dia	28.0	19.0	16.0	14.0	12.0	11.0	9.1	8.0
160 mm i/dia	76.0	53.0	43.0	37.0	33.0	29.0	25.0	22.0
200 mm i/dia	140.0	95.0	76.0	66.0	58.0	53.0	46.0	40.0

undesirable to lay small pipes at a shallower gradient than 1:40, as any ground settlement may reduce the gradient to an unacceptable level.

Pipeline materials

The choice of material for pipelines depends on the type of subsoil and the loading expected on the surface; the choice of size depends on the run-off expected. There are four possible materials; vitrified rigid clay pipes, ductile iron pipes, rigid concrete pipes, or flexible plastic pipes (see Figure 6.4).

Vitrified clay

The traditional thick clay pipes with heavy walls and large joints have largely been replaced by vitrified clay pipes. Vitrified clay is a very hard chemical resistant material, composed of carefully selected and processed clay fired to a high temperature; combined with rubber or plastic jointing it makes an impermeable drain very useful where oil, petrol or chemicals are likely to find their way into surface water drains. The pipes are rigid and can be broken by hard blows, but they have good load bearing properties, as they cannot be squashed by heavy lorries, though the bedding must be strong enough to prevent fracturing by settlement. Their weakness lies in the need for well-made joints which can otherwise be penetrated by tree roots.

They are controlled by British Standard BS EN 295 Part 1; they are made in a range of sizes and lengths:

DN 100 mm diameter x any length
DN 150 mm diameter x any length
DN 200 mm diameter x 1500, 2000 mm long
DN 225 mm diameter x 1500, 1750, 2000 mm long
DN 250 mm diameter x 1500, 2000 mm long
DN 300 mm diameter x 1500, 2000, 2500 mm long

Larger sizes are available but these are unlikely to be needed in landscape work.

Ductile iron

Iron pipes to BS 437 used to be made of grey cast iron, which was strong, had fewer joints than clay pipes, but was liable to corrosion and could be easily fractured. Modern iron pipes to BS EN 598 are made of ductile iron which is much tougher and less liable to fracture besides being lighter to handle, but their light section means that they should be treated as flexible pipes and bedded accordingly. They are really intended for water supplies under pressure, but there may be occasions when surface water needs to be run in pressure resistant pipes, and ductile iron is the best material for this purpose.

They can also be used where there is a danger of subsidence from traffic loading, since rigid concrete pipes are rather more liable to fracture. These pipes are controlled by BS EN 598, and the most suitable type for drainage work are pipes, ranging from 5.5 to 8.0 m long, with spigot and socket joints with a flexible connection which allows the pipeline to bend slightly without disaster. The pipes are obviously more expensive than plastic pipes, but the cost may be justifiable where plastic pipes could be crushed and where concrete pipes could fracture.

These pipes may be cement mortar or bitumen lined for special applications such as natural gas. They must be marked with the BS number, class number, manufacturer, date of manufacture and the size.

Table 6.4
Pipes to BS EN–598. Flexible joints for surface water drainage

5500 mm or 8000 mm long

80 mm bore	400 mm bore	1000 mm bore
100	450	1100
125		
150	500	1200
200	600	1400
250	700	1600
300	800	
350	900	

Rigid concrete pipes

These are specified in BS 5911: Part 100. They are used for many purposes in landscape and civil engineering work, from small drains of 150 mm diameter, through the one metre diameter sizes used for soakaways, silt pits, manholes and badger creeps, to the crane-handled three metre diameter pipes used for culverting, tunnels and water storage. The small units are made in plain concrete, while the larger sizes are reinforced with steel hoops and cages, and the pipes can be supplied with perforated sides to BS 5911: Part 114 to act as soakaways. Joints can be made with flexible material to accommodate slight earth movement, and ogee pipes to BS 5911: Part 110 give a stronger joint. Some of the more useful sizes for surface water drainage are:

DN 150 mm diameter × 450 to 3000 mm long
DN 225 mm diameter × 450 to 3000 mm long
DN 300 mm diameter × 450 to 3000 mm long
DN 375 mm diameter × 450 to 3000 mm long
DN 450 mm diameter × 450 to 3000 mm long

Flexible plastic pipes

Flexible plastic pipes have the great advantage that they can be laid in long runs without joints and can be laid easily round bends without the need for special curved units, but they can be squashed by heavy loads and can be punctured by digging equipment or even garden forks. An additional protection against damage to pipelines is to lay special 'marker tape' about 150 mm above the pipe, so that this is visible before the pipe is reached; some tapes include a metal strip which can be detected by electronic scanning equipment. If there is a particular stretch of piping where damage is likely to occur, concrete edging slabs or paving flags should be laid above the pipe to prevent accidental perforation. Two types of plastic pipe are suitable for surface water drains; PVC-U pipe to BS 4660 which is used for drainage around buildings, and Ultra-Rib PVC-U pipe to BS *Water Industry Standard* (WIS) 4-31-05 which is reinforced by concentric ribs to give extra strength equivalent to clay or concrete pipes for use where heavy loading is expected. All types of pipe are manufactured with a requisite range of bends, junctions, access points and connections; adaptors are available for different types of pipe.

Bedding of pipes generally

Almost more important than the choice of pipe material is the selection of the correct bedding for the pipeline. This depends on the type of pipe, the ground conditions, and the expected loading on the surface. Pipes may have to be laid quite close to the surface if the connections to the main drain are shallow, but where agricultural operations are likely to occur, pipes should be laid below 600 mm, which is the normal depth for ploughing. This 600 mm depth is also the

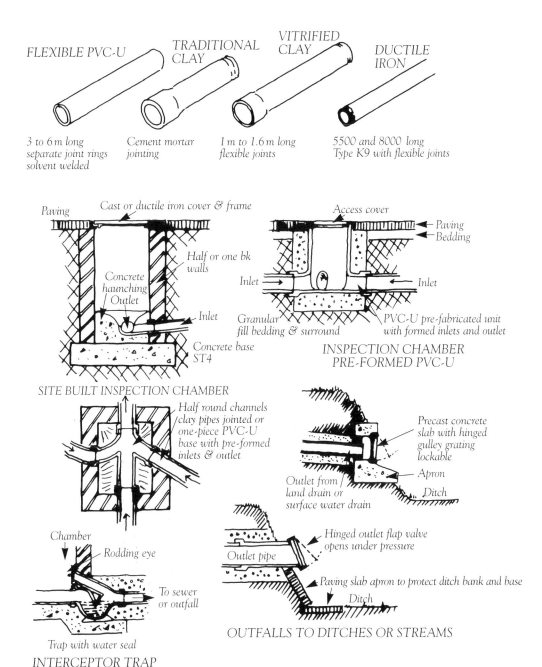

FLEXIBLE PVC-U
3 to 6 m long
separate joint rings
solvent welded

TRADITIONAL CLAY
Cement mortar jointing

VITRIFIED CLAY
1 m to 1.6 m long
flexible joints

DUCTILE IRON
5500 and 8000 long
Type K9 with flexible joints

Paving
Cast or ductile iron cover & frame
Concrete haunching
Outlet
Half or one bk walls
Inlet
Concrete base ST4

SITE BUILT INSPECTION CHAMBER

Access cover
Paving
Bedding
Inlet
Inlet
Granular fill bedding & surround
PVC-U pre-fabricated unit with formed inlets and outlet

INSPECTION CHAMBER
PRE-FORMED PVC-U

Half round channels clay pipes jointed or one-piece PVC-U base with pre-formed inlets & outlet

Precast concrete slab with hinged gulley grating lockable
Apron
Outlet from land drain or surface water drain
Ditch

Chamber
Rodding eye
To sewer or outfall
Trap with water seal
INTERCEPTOR TRAP

Hinged outlet flap valve opens under pressure
Outlet pipe
Paving slab apron to protect ditch bank and base
Ditch

OUTFALLS TO DITCHES OR STREAMS

Figure 6.4   Pipes and disposal of water

139

minimum level for frost free pipelines, and it is the maximum allowable depth for ground disturbance (without permission) in Areas of Archaeological Importance. Any soft spots or holes in the bottom of the trench must be cleaned out and packed with well-rammed granular fill or weak concrete to match the properties of the natural ground as far as possible. Particular care in bedding is needed where pipelines cross from one type of ground to another, and special flexible sections are available for rigid pipes where connections have to be made at these difficult points.

Bedding rigid clay or concrete pipes
Where the natural ground is suitable these pipes may be bedded on the bottom of the trench which must therefore be accurately cut to the fall of the pipeline; this is only practicable in firm undisturbed soil where an experienced workforce is employed. In most cases the pipes will have to be laid on various types of bedding according to the nature of the ground and the expected loading; the recommended bedding materials are:

- Under roadways, vehicle overrun on paving, or loading areas
  for pipe size DN 100 (minimum bore 96 mm)
      depth below finished surface of roadway to top of pipe:
      700 mm minimum to 4100 mm maximum, use class D
      500 mm minimum to 1800 mm maximum, use class F
      less than 500 mm, use solid concrete surround
  for pipe size DN 150 (minimum bore 146 mm)
      depth below finished surface of roadway to top of pipe:
      1100 mm minimum to 2500 mm maximum, use class D
      700 mm minimum to 3800 mm maximum, use class F
      less than 700 mm, use solid concrete surround
- Under 'pedestrian only' areas
  for pipe size DN 100
      depth below finished surface of roadway to top of pipe:
      400 mm minimum to 4200 mm maximum, use class D
      300 mm minimum to 5800 mm maximum, use class F
      less than 300 mm use solid concrete surround
  for pipe size DN 150
      depth below finished surface of roadway to top of pipe:
      600 mm minimum to 2500 mm maximum, use class D
      600 mm minimum to 3900 mm maximum, use class F
      less than 600 mm use solid concrete surround

DN sizes are convenient round figures expressing the internal diameter of the pipe without taking note of manufacturer's variations.

The classes of bedding for rigid clay or concrete pipes are given below and examples are shown in Figure 6.5.

- *Class D*: pipe laid on natural ground with cut-outs for joints, soil screened to remove stones over 40 mm and returned over pipe to 150 mm minimum depth. Suitable for firm ground with trenches trimmed by hand.
- *Class N*: pipe laid on 50 mm granular material of graded aggregate to Table 4 of BS 882, or 10 mm aggregate to Table 6 of BS 882, or as dug light soil (not clay) screened to remove stones over 10 mm. Suitable for machine dug trenches.
- *Class B*: as Class N, but with granular bedding extending half way up the pipe diameter.
- *Class F*: pipe laid on 100 mm granular fill to BS 882 below pipe, minimum 150 mm granular material fill above pipe: single size material. Suitable for machine dug trenches.
   - Use 10 mm granular material for 100 mm pipes;
   - Use 10 or 14 mm granular material for 150 mm pipes;
   - Use 10, 14, 20 mm granular material for 200–300 mm pipes;
   - Use 14 or 20 mm granular material for 375–500 mm pipes.
- *Class A*: concrete 100 mm thick under the pipe and reaching up to its middle, backfilled with the appropriate class of fill. This is used where there is only a very shallow fall to the drain, and the alignment of the pipes is important, since class A bedding allows the pipes to be laid to an exact gradient.
- *Concrete surround*: 25 mm sand blinding to bottom of trench, pipe supported on chocks, 100 mm concrete under the pipe, 150 mm concrete over the pipe. It is preferable to bed pipes under slabs or wall in granular material if this is feasible, since any subsidence in the building can be taken up by the granular material. The landscape designer should consult the architect for the type of bedding needed in a particular situation.

Bedding flexible plastic pipes

Typical examples of suitable bedding for flexible pipes under various conditions are shown in Figure 6.5. Provided that the conditions in which they are to be laid are suitable, flexible plastic pipes may be bedded on 'as dug' material. BS 5955: Part 6 requires as dug material to be generally less than 20 mm diameter; nothing should be over 38 mm, and not more than 5 per cent should be over 19 mm. It must be free of sharp particles which could damage the pipe. It should not be solid clay or chalk, but a good granular material which will pack down well on the pipe and fill all cavities in the trench. If such material is not available on site, granular fill will have to be imported, and this must be under 20 mm, composed of clean sharp sand, broken stone, gravel, quarry waste, or similar material. Unless solid concrete bedding is specified all flexible plastic pipe bedding must be:

- not less than 100 mm thick under the pipe;
- not less than 75 mm thick over the pipe (thicker cover must be placed in 75 mm layers);
- filled to the sides of the trench;

- compacted but not rammed down;
- in very soft 'runny' ground with fine particles the trench should be lined with geotextile filter fabric to retain the bedding in its proper place.

According to the type of soil and the expected loading, the bedding method should comply with BS 5955: Part 6, which gives recommendations for various ground conditions and loading:

1. Stable ground (rock, gravel, sand, clay, sandy clay)
a. under roadways, vehicle overrun on paving, or loading areas
    depth below finished surface of roadway to top of pipe:
        900 mm minimum to 1200 mm maximum, use Type 1
        1200 mm minimum to 6000 mm maximum, use Type 2
b. under 'pedestrian only' areas
    depth below finished surface of paving to top of pipe:
        less than 600 mm, use Type 3
        600 mm minimum to 6000 mm maximum, use Type 2
2. Unstable ground (sand, silty/clayey sand, silt, clay, sandy/silty clay)
a. under roadways, vehicle overrun on paving, or loading areas
    depth below finished surface of roadway to top of pipe:
        900 mm minimum to 1200 mm maximum, use Type 1
        1200 mm minimum to 2000 mm maximum, use Type 2
        below 2000 mm, use Type 4
        below 2000 mm minimum to 3000 m maximum, use Type 5
b. under 'pedestrian only' areas
    depth below finished surface of paving to top of pipe:
        less than 600 mm, use Type 3 if protection to pipe is necessary
        down to 2000 mm, use Type 2
        below 2000 mm, use Type 4
        below 2000 mm minimum to 3000 mm maximum, use Type 5

The types of bedding are as follows:

Type 1 = 100 mm fill below pipe, 300 mm above pipe: single size material
Type 2 = 100 mm fill below pipe, 300 mm above pipe: single size or graded material
Type 3 = 100 mm fill below pipe, 75 mm above pipe with concrete protective slab over
Type 4 = 100 mm fill below pipe, fill laid level with top of pipe
Type 5 = 200 mm fill below pipe, fill laid level with top of pipe
Solid concrete = 25 mm sand blinding to bottom of trench, pipe supported on chocks, 100 mm concrete under pipe, 150 mm concrete over pipe.

This method should be used where pipes pass close to buildings or walls, and the pipe trench might make the wall unstable. If the side of the pipe trench is less than

1 m from the foundation of a wall, Building Regulations require that the pipe be bedded in concrete to the level of the underside of the wall foundation. For pipe trenches further away from the building, the bedding will depend on local soil conditions and the Building Control Authority should be consulted.

Where pipes are bedded in concrete, the concrete must be gently vibrated into place, not rammed down, and allowed to set before the trench is backfilled. Plastic pipes are quite likely to float in liquid concrete, so they should be filled with water to hold them down before the concrete is poured. There is a tendency for the contractor to use any old concrete for this job, as with luck it will be covered up before the site is inspected, but obviously broken pipes under walls are expensive and difficult to repair, so it is important to make sure that this work is carried out properly. There will be some occasions where pipes have to pass under the walls of buildings, and Building Regulations may require that a space of 50 mm should be left round the pipe to allow for differential settlement. This opening must be protected from the entry of vermin by non-corrodible small diameter mesh.

Backfilling trenches for flexible pipes

The pipe trench must be backfilled in layers not exceeding 300 mm, and where the pipe is less than the prescribed distance below the surface, a concrete slab should be laid over the first 75 mm of fill so that machinery cannot damage it. There is a very complex formula known as 'Spangler's Iowa Formula' involving 26 factors and a large part of the Greek alphabet; this is used when the exact loading and stresses on a pipeline have to be calculated, but it is only necessary when heavy traffic is running over sewer pipes, and should not normally be required in a landscape contract. If landscape work does involve heavy vehicles moving over pipelines, it is advisable to consult a civil engineer or drainage engineer.

Gulleys and access points

Channels must discharge into pipelines at regular intervals so that the water does not build up into a large flow before being removed. The discharge may be collected from the paving by several means such as:

- individual trapped gulleys with removable but lockable gratings;
- continuous gratings over precast concrete channels;
- kerb outlets which are constructed as part of the concrete kerb line;
- in more rural areas, by a concrete outfall into a ditch or stream.

Examples are shown in Figures 6.2, 6.3 and 6.4.

The spacing of gulleys depends on the gradient of the paving and the amount of run-off to be collected, and where the gulleys also serve as access points for cleaning, the length of the drain cleaning rods is a factor, as drains must be easily accessible for regular cleaning and for emergency clearance of blockages.

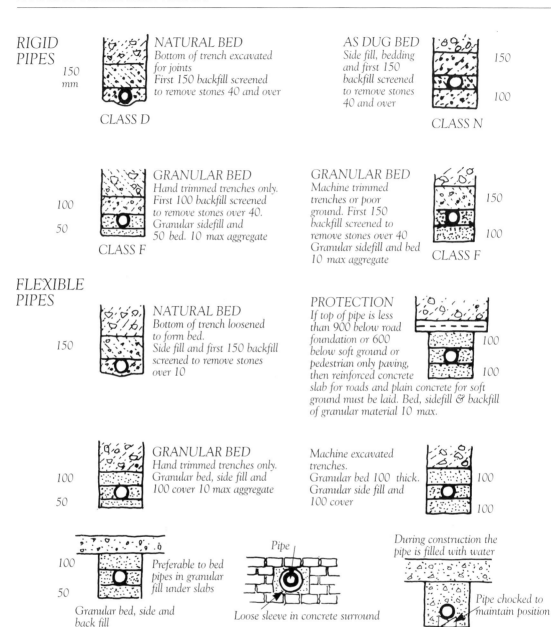

RIGID PIPES
150 mm

NATURAL BED
Bottom of trench excavated for joints
First 150 backfill screened to remove stones 40 and over

CLASS D

AS DUG BED
Side fill, bedding and first 150 backfill screened to remove stones 40 and over
150
100

CLASS N

100
50

GRANULAR BED
Hand trimmed trenches only.
First 100 backfill screened to remove stones over 40.
Granular sidefill and 50 bed. 10 max aggregate

CLASS F

GRANULAR BED
Machine trimmed trenches or poor ground. First 150 backfill screened to remove stones over 40 Granular sidefill and bed 10 max aggregate
150
100

CLASS F

FLEXIBLE PIPES

150

NATURAL BED
Bottom of trench loosened to form bed.
Side fill and first 150 backfill screened to remove stones over 10

PROTECTION
If top of pipe is less than 900 below road foundation or 600 below soft ground or pedestrian only paving, then reinforced concrete slab for roads and plain concrete for soft ground must be laid. Bed, sidefill & backfill of granular material 10 max.
100
100

100
50

GRANULAR BED
Hand trimmed trenches only.
Granular bed, side fill and 100 cover 10 max aggregate

Machine excavated trenches.
Granular bed 100 thick.
Granular side fill and 100 cover
100
100

100
50

Preferable to bed pipes in granular fill under slabs

Granular bed, side and back fill

CONCRETE SLAB

Pipe

Loose sleeve in concrete surround

PIPE THROUGH WALL

During construction the pipe is filled with water

Pipe chocked to maintain position

CONCRETE SLAB

Figure 6.5   Drainage pipe bedding

The run-off as calculated above will give the amount of water to be collected, and the size of the discharge pipe will be ascertained from this figure; ideally the gulleys should be so spaced that each gulley takes half or less than the full amount of run-off so that in the event of one gulley becoming blocked the next gulley will be able to cope. If the paving layout and the cost of the job permits, no area should be served by only one gulley. For access purposes the maximum length of pipe without an access point should be not more than that shown in Table 6.5.

Table 6.5
Maximum distance between access points

From head of drain:	to any access point	12 m
	to inspection chamber	22 m
	to manhole	45 m
From rodding eye:	to access point or junction	22 m
	to inspection chamber or manhole	45 m
From small access point:	to junction	22 m
	to inspection chamber or manhole	45 m
From inspection chamber:	to inspection chamber	45 m
From manhole:	to manhole	90 m

Gulleys should never be placed right in the middle of footways or in front of doors or gates, and not in line with pedestrian crossings or car park entrances. All these locations are at risk from ponding if gulleys become blocked, and there is also a risk of shoe heels, wheelchairs, pram wheels, trolley wheels and umbrellas becoming trapped in the gulley gratings. If possible, gulleys should not be placed where litter, road sweepings, leaves or other detritus is likely to accumulate as it is extremely tempting for the road sweeper to shovel the rubbish into the gulley rather than to pick it up; if this cannot be avoided it is advisable to increase the number of gulleys.

Only too often the number of access points to a drainage system – rodding eyes, manholes, inspection junctions and gulleys – are limited by cost or lack of foresight, and the consequent annoying blockages, excavation and expense can easily be avoided by providing just a few more access points in the first place. Every length of drain should be accessible, since even if no blockage is expected to occur in the normal life of the project, later contractors may well sweep rubbish into the nearest drain point. An example of an inspection chamber and an interceptor trap are shown in Figure 6.4.

Disposal of surface water

The water from the pipeline eventually discharges either into the main foul sewer system, or in more enlightened areas into a 'surface water only' drainage system where it can be used in ornamental lakes. All surface water and foul drains must pass through an interceptor chamber before they are allowed to discharge into a

Plate 26 *Road gulley set neatly into channel and paving pattern. The sharp angled corners of some blocks have been chipped by traffic; it is preferable to use squared blocks wherever possible. Wakefield Cathedral precinct paving design by Tess Jaray. (Photograph by courtesy of Terry Knight Consultancy.)*

public sewer. An interceptor chamber is similar to an ordinary manhole but with a trapped bend at the outlet which provides a water seal against smells, gases and vermin entering the drainage system from the sewer. The interceptor trap is fitted with a rodding eye to allow the length between the sewer and the interceptor chamber to be cleaned (see Figure 6.4).

Where there is a risk of chemicals, petrol, grease or oil entering the drainage system, various types of special interceptor chambers must be provided, but these are not normally part of the landscape contract, since foul water drainage and sewerage are covered in the building contract. Normal car parking of modern cars does not produce enough pollutants to harm the drainage system, but where vehicle washing or spillage from industrial and garage work occurs, interceptors must be provided, and the effluent must go into a foul sewer and not into a surface water or land drain. The law requires the disposal of trade effluents to be specially licensed.

For small domestic surface water drainage and land drainage, a soakaway is adequate where this is permitted by the local authority, and unless the run-off is contaminated by petrol or other chemicals, it can be discharged into an ornamental pond with the pond overflow draining into a soakaway. Where the existing public surface water drainage system is already fully loaded, the local authority may require all surface water to be taken to a soakaway. In projects where ornamental water features are part of the design they may be anything from a small pond in a private garden to a large lake in a complex development such as a university, hospital or business park. These not only enhance the design but will also act as 'balancing ponds' which cope with excess ground and surface water thereby reducing the load on the sewerage system. If this system is used the landscape designer must be careful to see that the pond edges look attractive whatever the water level. The ponds used to collect heavy run-off from highways are sometimes referred to as 'pollution control ponds' and this implies that the landscape designer should be careful not to allow run-off from car parks or other polluted water to enter an ecologically healthy pond.

Outfalls to watercourses

The outlet or 'outfall' of the collecting drain is a precast or in situ concrete unit which is designed to prevent erosion of the watercourse and to stop earth and vegetation from blocking the mouth of the drain. The outfall also serves to mark the position of the drain, as machine clearance of watercourses could easily destroy the pipe mouth if it were hidden by vegetation. Examples of outfalls are shown in Figure 6.4.

6.3 LAND DRAINAGE

Land drainage of sub-strate

When dealing with the drainage of any water-holding sub-strate it is important to look at the problem as a whole from the sub-strate to the finished paving surface. The type of drainage will depend upon the composition of the sub-strate. If the sub-strate is composed of a comparatively impermeable soil such as clay, it may be necessary to install land drains below the base in order to prevent the paving from becoming waterlogged and thereby losing its strength and integrity. This is particularly important in the case of granular paving, open-jointed sand-bedded pavers or flags, and block paving, where saturated ground could result in the surface subsiding and ponding after heavy rain, becoming soft and incapable of carrying traffic, or even breaking up. The viability of the grass in grass concrete paving may be affected by waterlogging of the sub-strate, which can cause the grass to subside below the concrete units.

The calculation of the rainfall entering land drains from a given area is described in Section 6.2, Calculation of Paving Drainage, and for practical purposes it may be assumed that all the rain falling on granular paving permeates to the base. The spacing and sizing of land drains can then be designed to remove all the rainfall without ponding.

Table 6.6	
Permeability of soils	
Soil type	Drainage capability
Boulders and cobbles	good
Hardcore	
broken stone, brick	excellent
chalk, soft rock	fair to poor
Gravel	
well graded (no fines)	excellent
with fines	fair to poor
Sand	
well graded (no fines)	excellent
with fines	fair to poor
Silt	poor
Clay	
low plasticity	very poor
moderate plasticity	fair to bad
high plasticity	bad
Peat	fair to poor

A land drainage system for a large area usually consists of a herring-bone pattern composed of 'laterals' or side drains giving into a main 'spine' drain which directs the water to an outlet such as a French drain, ditch or surface water drain; in small areas the drains discharge directly into a final disposal point. Some typical land drainage patterns are shown in Figure 6.7. Spacing of land drains varies from 3 m in heavy clay soils to 18 m for very permeable soils, with a minimum fall of 1 in 200. Where the land drain discharges into a soakaway or main drain, a 'catchpit' or 'siltpit' must be provided; this traps the silt before the water enters the drain or soakaway. The depth of the pit below the land drain invert must be at least 300 mm. It will have to be cleaned out at regular intervals, and therefore it must be built in the manner of a manhole with a removable cover (suitable for the traffic conditions) and clearly marked.

Land drains may be clayware, concrete, glass composite or flexible plastic piping: typical examples are shown in Figure 6.6. Unglazed clayware field drain pipes are made in short lengths and are specified in BS 1196; they are usually 75 mm or 100 mm in diameter, laid dry with open joints through which the water percolates. Porous concrete pipes to BS 5911: Part 114 are similar in size and installation. Perforated corrugated flexible plastic piping is controlled by BS 4962; these pipes are much lighter than clay or concrete, and they can be laid from a continuous roll by hand or machine. In deciding which type of pipe to use, the size of the area to be drained is an important factor as the short lengths of clay or concrete pipe make them easier to handle in small enclosed areas, while machine laid plastic piping is better suited to large areas such as sports fields and car parks. It is also worth remembering that clay pipes can carry 50 per cent more water than perforated plastic pipes, as the corrugated surface of plastic piping has great hydraulic friction, and that plastic piping cannot be laid in temperatures below freezing. Some of the water will drain along the outside of the pipe, and the flow inside the pipe has the effect of drawing the ground water towards the pipe.

Whichever type is specified, the piping should be laid in dry conditions when a proper bed can be formed; this bed is usually the natural bottom of the trench. Backfilling may be returned soil if this is evenly graded granular material under 20 mm, or in less porous soils a better method is to use imported granular material to form a good porous layer round the pipes. Unless the material surrounding the pipe permits the water to flow freely into the pipe, the system will not function; if the fill contains very fine particles the pipe should be filter-wrapped with a geotextile material to prevent these particles from being washed into the drain and thereby creating voids in the backfill which may cause subsidence in the paving surface (see Figure 6.6).

Clayware field drains

Also known as agricultural drain pipes or land drain pipes. Clayware pipes are plain ended without joints, made in standard sizes:

DN   75 mm diameter × 305 mm long
DN 100 mm diameter × 305 mm long
DN 150 mm diameter × 305 mm long
DN 225 mm diameter × 305, 450 and 600 mm long
DN 300 mm diameter × 305, 450 and 600 mm long

Junctions and other special shapes can be manufactured. The water percolates through the open joints between pipes, which is satisfactory in coarse textured soils, but in fine sandy soils the pipes should be wrapped in filter fabric to keep the fine particles out.

Concrete pipes

Porous concrete pipes are specified in BS 5911: Part 114. They are made in lengths from 450 to 1250 mm; available diameters are shown in Table 6.7. They can be plain ended or with ogee joints (specified in BS 5911: Part 110) to make a firmer connection. These pipes can be made fully porous, or with the bottom third non-porous so that only water from above will enter the pipe. They can be made either with ordinary Portland cement or with sulphate resisting cement (pipe marked blue) for use in high sulphate soils.

Glass composite pipes

Somewhat stronger than plain concrete pipes are the glass rovings reinforced concrete (GRC) pipes made to BS 5911: Part 101. Bends and junctions are made to match; surprisingly, the bends are formed of linked short straight lengths rather than curves, which seems an odd way of going round a corner. They are made in three

Table 6.7
Porous concrete pipes to BS 5911: Part 114

Diameter in mm	Infiltration rate in litres/second/metre run
DN 100	1.08
DN 150	1.67
DN 225	2.50
DN 300	3.33
DN 375	4.17
DN 450	4.17
DN 525	4.17
DN 600	4.17
DN 750	4.17
DN 900	4.17

strengths, Class L, Class M, and Class N. Class N is the strongest. The sizes of these pipes are similar to plain concrete pipes. These pipes are useful where the loading on the paved area is unknown, where the sub-strate is dubious, or where the main contractor is likely to run heavy plant over the area after the drains have been laid.

Plastic pipes
Perforated PVC-U plastic pipes are controlled by BS 4962. They must be laid not less than 600 mm below the finished paving surface, and the bedding may be on the natural bottom of the trench with the pipe laid in a shallow groove in the bottom. If the soil is not suitable for forming a groove, the pipe must be bedded in granular material laid up to its middle. Perforated pipe must not be laid within 5 m of trees; a short length of unperforated pipe must be used for these areas as otherwise tree roots will seek out the holes in order to get at the water in the pipe. The amount of water the pipes can handle depends on the pressure of the groundwater; some normal values are shown in Table 6.8.

Table 6.8
Discharge capacity of flexible ribbed perforated plastic pipes

Hydraulic gradient (%)	Discharge capacity of pipe in litres/second:			
	60 mm	80 mm	100 mm	125 mm diameter
0.5	0.8	1.6	3.3	5.9
1.0	1.1	2.2	4.3	7.4
2.0	1.4	2.9	5.8	10.0
3.0	1.8	3.5	7.0	12.0

Catchwater drains
Although these drains are not properly part of a paving design, they may sometimes be used for surface water disposal in open landscape projects.

Catchwater drains are vertical interceptor drains which cut off water flowing either on or under the paving and prevent it from percolating into adjoining areas, or alternatively they catch water flowing towards the paving and prevent it from saturating the paving sub-base. They are frequently used to catch the run-off from roads or paved areas; to reduce water pressure behind a retaining wall, or to form a barrier in permeable soil; they are not suitable for taking large point discharges from main surface water drains, as their function is to remove water slowly and continually rather than rapidly. Catchwater drains are fairly cheap, so if there is any uncertainty about future alterations to the landscape which might affect ground water movement, it is better to install extra drainage at the beginning rather than to wait for an angry and waterlogged client to demand an instant remedy. One advantage of catchwater drains is that they can be grassed or gravelled over a geotextile layer to give continuity to the landscape. Catchwater drains are usually taken down to a depth where the ground water can no longer affect the paving or the soil structure. They are designed to discharge into natural or man-made watercourses, not into sewers, so while the bottom of the catchwater drain must be lower than the land drains discharging into it, or the base of the paving at least, the final discharge of the drain must not be less than 150 mm above the highest likely water level of the stream or ditch which takes the outfall. There are three types of catchwater drains, and all types should be capped with a geotextile layer to prevent fine material from being washed into the drain, and finished with gravel, ballast or other permeable material appropriate to the paving.

Rubble drain
The simplest type of catchwater drain is a 'rubble' drain consisting of a trench filled with 20–75 mm rough broken stone, gravel or hardcore, topped with geotextile and grass or gravel.

French drain
The more effective 'French drain' has a clay, concrete or perforated plastic land drain pipe at the bottom of a trench filled with granular material and topped with geotextile and grass, gravel, or open-jointed paving. In fine soils, geotextile material may be used to line the sides and bottom of the trench to prevent particles from clogging the drain.

Fin drain
The most sophisticated type of catchwater drain is called a 'fin drain' or 'sheet drain' and in addition to the land drain at the bottom it is provided with special vertical geotextile material which helps to collect the water and to lead it more rapidly to its discharge point. The sheet drain may be laid in a slot by itself, or it may be laid on the downhill side of an ordinary French drain, but it should not be used where soil cultivation is likely to disturb it (see Figure 6.6). Standard drains

of this type are suitable for depths up to 2 m, but special versions are manufactured for deeper applications in civil engineering where earthworks and foundations must be kept in a stable condition.

The basic type consists of two porous geotextile fabrics bonded to each side of a more open textured water conducting layer which leads the groundwater rapidly and cleanly to a land drain pipe at the foot, where the fabric is wrapped round the pipe to prevent soil particles from blocking the drain. An average flow capacity for such a drain with a 100 mm pipe would be about 1.60 litres/second/metre for the vertical component. These sheet drains can also be carried under granular paving to provide horizontal drainage directing the water more effectively into the vertical drain, though a heavier type is necessary to prevent the material from being squashed by traffic.

A more complex sheet drain is designed for situations where the groundwater must be cut off more absolutely than is possible with an ordinary drain, such as water percolating down a slope towards a building where the foundations must be protected from groundwater, and where no ponding or flooding can be permitted. The vertical 'fin' or 'sheet' is composed of two layers; a waterproof membrane adjoining the area to be protected, and a drainage layer of vertical porous material on the uphill side which conducts the water to the foot. These two layers are usually bonded together, though they can be laid separately. The composite sheet is wrapped round a perforated plastic land drain at the foot, where it acts as a geotextile filter to prevent soil particles from entering the drain.

Mole drainage

In heavy clay ground a simple type of drain can be made with a 'mole plough' which has a steel cone at the bottom of a narrow blade. This is dragged through the clay, forming a hole which retains its shape sufficiently well to drain the soil; though the mole ploughing must be repeated at regular intervals, and the hole can be closed by heavy traffic on the surface. Small diameter flexible perforated pipes can be laid in the same way by pulling the pipe through a slit opened up in the ground which closes itself after the pipe has passed through. This method is satisfactory for land drains in open homogeneous ground, but should not be used for surface water drains near buildings where tree roots, old foundations and other obstructions are found.

Sand slitting

This is a very simple method of draining the turf layer of grassed areas, and is not really related to paving, though it is useful for drying out damp areas adjoining paving where pedestrians may walk. Machine sand slitting is done in a single operation by means of a vibrating blade which cuts a slot 300 mm deep and 40–80 mm wide, while a hopper fills the slot first with gravel and then with fine sand; the slot is then closed by a roller. For manual sand slitting, slots are cut in the turf about 200 mm deep in a herring-bone pattern directed towards the lowest

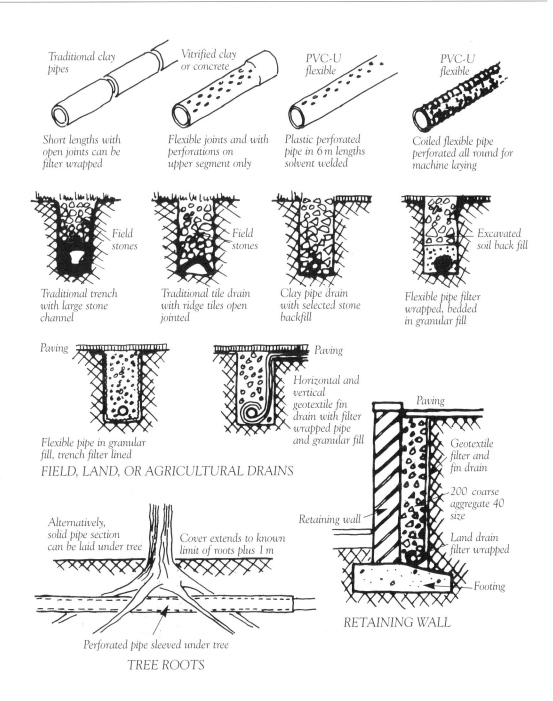

Traditional clay pipes

Short lengths with open joints can be filter wrapped

Vitrified clay or concrete

Flexible joints and with perforations on upper segment only

PVC-U flexible

Plastic perforated pipe in 6 m lengths solvent welded

PVC-U flexible

Coiled flexible pipe perforated all round for machine laying

Field stones

Traditional trench with large stone channel

Field stones

Traditional tile drain with ridge tiles open jointed

Clay pipe drain with selected stone backfill

Excavated soil back fill

Flexible pipe filter wrapped, bedded in granular fill

Paving

Flexible pipe in granular fill, trench filter lined

Paving

Horizontal and vertical geotextile fin drain with filter wrapped pipe and granular fill

FIELD, LAND, OR AGRICULTURAL DRAINS

Paving

Geotextile filter and fin drain

200 coarse aggregate 40 size

Retaining wall

Land drain filter wrapped

Footing

RETAINING WALL

Alternatively, solid pipe section can be laid under tree

Cover extends to known limit of roots plus 1 m

Perforated pipe sleeved under tree

TREE ROOTS

Figure 6.6   Land drainage

point; the slots are cut with a sharp spade and filled with sharp sand or fine gravel (under 3 mm) to just below the surface. Although in good landscape work the soil structure should have been improved before the area was grassed, sand slitting is useful when dealing with existing waterlogged ground. It will have to be repeated at intervals as the sand becomes clogged with fine soil particles.

Soakaways

The construction of local or main sewerage is not discussed here as it is outside the normal work of the landscape designer, but the construction of small soakaways may often be part of the land drainage contract. These allow the surface water discharged into them to seep out into the surrounding ground. Traditionally, soakaways were built rather like wells – sometimes old wells were used for this purpose – with rings of brick or stone let down into the ground as the pit was dug from under them; these pits were subsequently filled with rubble. Soakaways can be either site-built or pre-fabricated. Examples of these are shown in Figure 6.7.

Foundations

In firm ground no foundation is needed for a small domestic soakaway, but in unstable or soft ground, and where large soakaways are installed, a plain concrete slab foundation 150 mm thick will be adequate. The type of concrete depends on the soil conditions as shown in Table 6.9.

Site-built soakaways

Two types of soakaways are recognized; circular and trench forms. Trench soakaways follow the contours and provide more capacity, as they can be any size, and have a greater surface for dispersal. It is not always possible to excavate a long trench and it is more difficult to find (for maintenance purposes) than a circular pit. Trench soakaways are more suitable for rural sites where there is not likely to be any ground disturbance, and size for size they offer better dispersal of water than a pit soakaway.

Site-built soakaways are less economical than pre-fabricated soakaways of concrete rings as they must be filled with rubble, thus providing 50 to 60 per cent less water capacity. Site-built soakaways are constructed of one brick thick walls,

Table 6.9 Concrete mixes for soakaway foundations		
Application	Standard mix	Designated mix
Mass concrete foundations in:		
non-aggressive soils	ST 4 (C20P)	GEN 4
mild sulphate soils		FND 2
bad sulphate soils		FND 3
very bad sulphate soils		FND 4

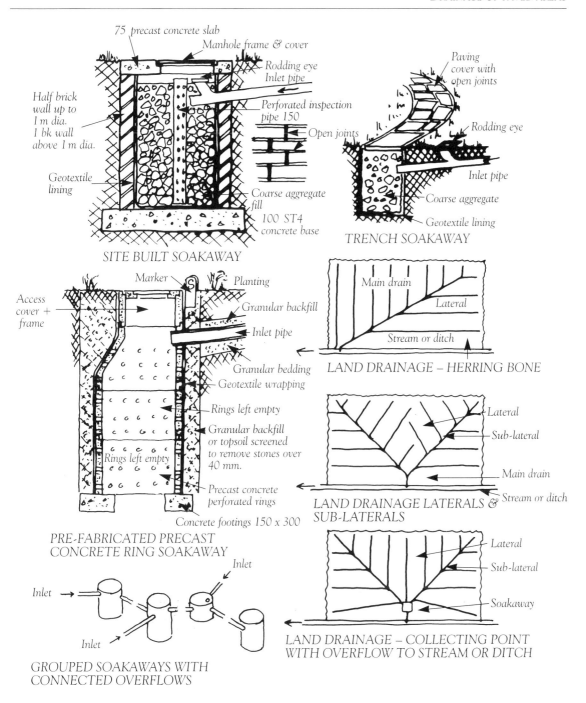

Figure 6.7   Soakaways

laid with mortar beds but with open vertical joints below 600 mm. Brick soakaways are filled with clean well broken brick or stone as an open-jointed brick wall is not strong enough to withstand the external soil pressure; the walls are set on a 500 × 150 mm concrete foundation and the base is constructed of 250 mm rammed hardcore. The top of the soakaway must be capped with an access cover, and an inspection pipe running to the bottom of the soakaway is fitted to allow the state of the filling to be examined and to provide a marker for the soakaway. This construction is illustrated in Figure 6.7. Soakaways must be sited away from buildings – the distance depends on the site conditions and the local Building Control Authority should be consulted. They should preferably be sited away from trees, as the collected rainwater offers a temptingly easy supply for thirsty roots, though unless the roots are likely to damage the walls of the soakaway they offer a good way of getting rid of the surplus water. Plants with large water requirements will be very happy growing next to soakaways as long as they can be watered in dry weather.

Pre-fabricated soakaways

Pre-fabricated soakaways are usually constructed with precast perforated concrete rings stacked to give the required capacity, and supplied complete with inlet pipes and covers. The covers should be specified as light, medium, or heavy duty according to the traffic they are likely to carry. Larger precast soakaways, or soakaways installed where there is limited access, can be constructed of special interlocking sections built to the specified diameter and depth. These precast soakaways are left empty, as they are self-supporting, and the outside should be surrounded by coarse geotextile filter fabric to prevent backfill from getting into the soakaway, and the excavation should be backfilled with granular material to allow free dispersal of water. Although the excellent Building Research Establishment (BRE) *Digest* No. 365 recommends that geotextile should not be placed outside the rings since it cannot be removed for cleaning, it seems unlikely that any client would take the trouble to change the geotextiles regularly, and consequently external geotextile is better than nothing. The construction of a pre-fabricated soakaway is shown in Figure 6.7. Soakaways in clay soil are not very practicable and it is advisable to test the draining ability of the soils before deciding on the use of soakaways and their capacity (which can easily be done by pouring a measured amount of water into suitably placed trial holes and noting the dispersal time). If the soil is not sufficiently permeable in itself, it may be necessary to provide dispersal pipes of perforated plastic or clay land drains laid to fall away from the lower part of the soakaway, though this may mean digging rather expensive deep trenches.

Some manufacturers make special precast concrete soakaway units ranging from 1.5 m diameter to 6.0 m diameter, but there is an advantage in connecting up several small soakaways rather than one big one, as inlets can be taken to each soakaway instead of all the water going into one pit, and if one gets full the overflow will go to the next pit and not all over the front drive. Precast concrete soakaways to BS 5911: Part 200 are made in the same way as manholes, but with perforated sides. There is a wide range of sizes, and the choice between a shallow wide pit and a narrow deep pit will depend on the permeability of the soil and the space available for the soakaway. Large diameter soakaways have tapered rings at the top so that a standard manhole cover can be fitted. Standard sizes for DN pipes (internal diameter) are:

Nominal sizes:
- shafts, 675, 900 mm;
- chambers, 900, 1050, 1200, 1350, 1500, 1800, 2100, 2400, 2700, 3000 mm.

The correct size can be calculated by a very complicated method described in BRE *Digest* No. 365 (which is not described here), or by the much simpler but quite satisfactory method of assuming a depth of 18 mm of water over the area to be drained and selecting a soakaway which contains this amount. The figure of 18 mm is in excess of the British Standard recommendations, but gives a tolerance which allows for unusually heavy rainfall, weeds in the soakaway, or delay in dispersing the water from the soakaway. The capacity is calculated to the invert of the inlet pipe, otherwise the water could flow back up the pipe with unpopular results. Thus for an area of 30 x 20 m the soakaway would need to hold:

$$30 \times 20 \times 0.018 = 10.83 \, \text{m}^3 \text{ of water.}$$
$$\text{Try soakaway 1.8 m diameter, then } \frac{10.83}{3.142 \times 0.9 \times 0.9} = 4.25 \, \text{m deep below invert}$$

A reasonable size for the JCB to lift is a ring 600 mm deep, so if the invert of the inlet pipe is 700 mm below ground level, seven 600 mm rings below invert level and one 600 mm ring plus a 100 mm precast concrete cover slab should be about right. This is a large soakaway, and it might be preferable to use several small soakaways rather than one large one, as this does not put too much load on any one soakaway, and does not overload the adjoining ground with water.

7 SPECIAL PAVING

There are a number of occasions when special consideration has to be given to the design and construction of paving and roadways, either because of site problems, or because of the special needs of the users. This section describes some of the most common situations.

7.1 DESIGN FOR THE DISABLED

The term 'disabled' covers people who are physically incapable of using steps, the blind and partially sighted, and elderly people who are not technically disabled but who need to feel that support is available when using paths and steps. Temporarily disabled people include over-enthusiastic skiers with plastered legs, people convalescent after major operations, and those with heavy or awkward loads, such as mothers with compound loads of a pram, two toddlers, and the week's shopping, or the DIY enthusiast with a pre-fabricated staircase. Although wheelchair access must be easily identified, the landscape designer should be competent to incorporate the needs of the disabled into the design without making conspicuous routes which signal that disabled people are 'different' from the rest of the people using the area.

There is a growing practice of including the disabled in all activities, even in the more strenuous sports, so the landscape designer should bear in mind some critical dimensions for access paths and roadways which should be incorporated in landscape projects where disabled people are likely to go. This means in practice that all projects should be designed with the disabled in mind.

Wheelchairs

Critical dimensions for manoeuvring wheelchairs are given below. Remember that the wheelchair is often pushed by a helper, so allow plenty of room. The minimum width really is minimum, while the preferred width allows easy clearance without risking a scrape (see Figure 7.1).

- absolute minimum width at a point obstacle   = 900 mm
  (bollard or lamp-post)
- preferred minimum width at a point obstacle   = 1350 mm
- absolute minimum width of footway   = 1800 mm
- preferred minimum width of footway   = 2000 mm
- preferred minimum width of footway at bus stops etc.   = 3000 mm
- preferred minimum width of footway at shop doors   = 3500 mm
- preferred maximum crossfall on paving   = 1:20
  (wheelchairs can tip over or run off on steep angles)
  with a steeper fall at each side.
- preferred maximum opening in tree grilles etc.   = 13 mm
  (walking aids get trapped, and slots should be
  at right angles to direction of travel)

Car parking for disabled drivers

The following dimensions are minimal (see Figure 7.1):

- single parking bay   = 3300 mm wide × 4800 mm long
- double bay sharing access space   = 6000 mm wide × 4800 mm long
- kerbside parking bay   = 6600 mm long
  (to allow for loading wheelchairs into the boot)

Regulations require that car parks must reserve marked places for disabled as follows:

- private car parks under 200 places must reserve 5 per cent with at least 2 places
- private car parks over 200 places must reserve 2 per cent plus 6 extra places
- public car parks under 200 places must reserve 6 per cent with at least 3 places
- public car parks over 200 places must reserve 4 per cent with at least 4 places

Disabled parking bays should be clearly marked both on the ground and by a vertical sign which can be seen from the entrance and which is big enough to embarrass illegal users.

Paths

It is good practice to provide raised edges 100 mm high for paths used by wheelchairs, as this stops them running off the path; it also acts as a guide for blind people or partially sighted people using guide sticks. It needs careful design to avoid a conflict with the requirements for mowing and sweeping paths, and also to allow free drainage of run-off water. There may be occasions where blind people

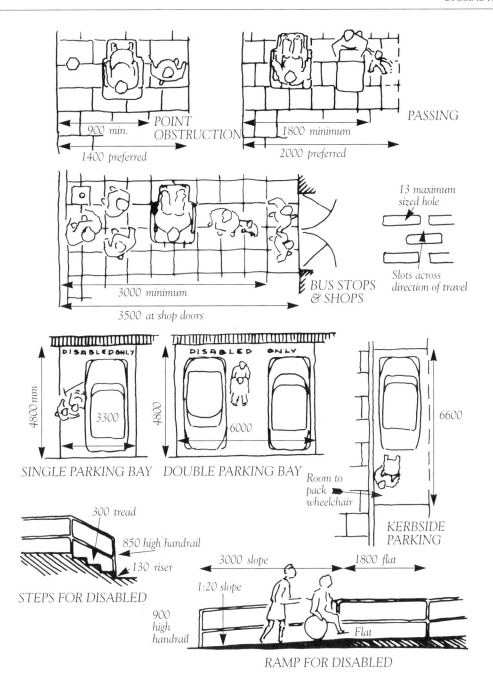

Figure 7.1   Paving for disabled users

and cyclists have to share a route, in which case they should be separated by a raised strip of thermoplastic material 12 mm high × 150 mm wide; corrugated tactile patches can be used at the start and end of the route – transversely for the blind, and longitudinally for the cyclists. Although cyclists are very unlikely to ride into blind people the almost silent passage of the cycle can frighten blind people.

Barriers and crossings

Pedestrian barriers should be designed with staggered openings at main junctions or schools to prevent runaway wheelchairs from getting out into the traffic; the openings should be not less than 1200 mm wide. Wheelchairs and lame people crossing side roads need dropped crossings the full width of the footway, but these should be marked by tactile slabs or offset from the line of the footway so that blind people do not walk into the side road without warning. Car parking should never be allowed to obstruct dropped kerbs. Much research has been done on the best pattern of tactile paving for blind people; it is important that they feel the surface clearly, and also remember the meaning of the pattern. Not surprisingly, the easiest surfaces to feel were the most uncomfortable to walk on, and several different patterns can be used to convey messages such as 'STEPS AHEAD', 'CROSS HERE', 'BUS STOP'. The Transport and Road Research Laboratory (TRRL) recommend five types of warning pattern:

- for crossings: concrete flag with flat topped blisters 4.5 mm high;
- for warnings of danger: concrete ribbed flags with ribs 75 mm apart;
- for platform edges: rubber tile with flat topped blisters 11.5 mm wide;
- for guidance through open space: rubber tile or concrete flag with bar pattern running in direction of travel;
- for bus stop: rubber tile.

Ramps and steps

Ramps must legally be provided for access to nearly all public buildings, and the following are the critical dimensions for their design (see Figure 7.1):

- slope not more than 1:20 with flat resting places at 6000 mm intervals;
- absolute maximum slope is 1:12 with a maximum length of 3000 mm;
- minimum width 1350 mm, with 2000 mm width where wheelchairs must pass each other or turn at right angles;
- handrails to ramp on both sides 900 mm high;
- steps for the disabled should be 1200 mm wide:
    risers 100–150 mm, 130 mm preferred,
    treads 300 mm wide with no nosing and 6 mm rounded arrises,
    maximum rise of flight 1200 mm with resting place 1200 × 1200 mm;
- handrails to steps on both sides 850 mm high.

Plate 27 *Tactile paving units at pedestrian crossing. The colour is pale buff, and is intended to indicate a non-controlled crossing to blind people.*

7.2 PLAYGROUNDS AND SPORTS AREAS

Hard porous surfaces

These surfaces are recommended by the National Playing Fields Association for athletics, hockey, tennis, junior football and for some practice and coaching areas; they are not recommended for cricket, rugby, soccer, netball, or basketball.

They are made of graded hard limestone, granite, crushed brick or shale (blaes) and depend on their ability to hold moisture and the structure of the particles for their stability; they are self-binding and unlike bitumen macadam they are not held together with a binder. Blaes or crushed stone from a local source can be used as a cheaper alternative. If this type of material is used no particles should be larger than 5 mm, though 3 mm is preferred. The specialist contractor may lay the base, or it may be laid by the landscape contractor; a typical base is formed of:

● DoT Type 1 fill, 10–25 mm graded material laid to fall, and compacted with 1.5 tonne roller,

163

- blinded with crushed stone, hard ash or sand 3–10 mm particles;
- finished surface laid with well graded broken stone or similar material, maximum size of particles 5 mm, finished thickness 150 mm, then
- compacted with a 1.5 tonne roller,
- watered to saturation point,
- drained,
- compacted again.

Manufacturers of special sports surfaces may require that their own base material is supplied and laid by them if the surface is to be guaranteed. The sub-contract is then for the complete system. It is essential that all sports likely to be played on the surface are covered in the specification, and the standard required, whether school, standard, competition, or international, is also specified, as the difference in cost is quite considerable, and with modern sports scores being measured in hundredths of a second the quality of the track can be critical to success or failure.

Whichever surface is used good drainage is the key to life expectancy on a well maintained and carefully used pitch, where the life expectancy can be as much as 25 years. Careful use includes not overusing the surface or using it when frosts have caused frost-heave, or when heavy rain has affected the drainage, and these considerations should be pointed out to the client before damage occurs.

The surfaces supplied and laid by specialist contractors vary considerably, but generally the construction must follow certain principles:

- Drains must be not less than 400 mm to invert with permeable backfill of broken stone or similar 38 to 12 mm, blinded with gravel or crushed stone 10–3mm to a depth of 50 mm to within 25 mm of the final surface. Connection to the main drain should be via a 900 x 600 mm silt pit 300 mm below the level of the outlet pipe. A perimeter land drain or catchwater drain should be provided to control the water level of the sports area.
- Irrigation may be needed, either by means of overhead watering or underground pipelines.
- Edgings should be provided at the sides of the sports area to contain the surface, but these should not impede the drainage.

Playgrounds

Nowadays playgrounds with play equipment are usually surfaced with a resilient material which reduces the effect of falls and accidents. There are many proprietary materials which are supplied and laid by specialist contractors; mainly rubber tiles or sheet material on a hard base such as bitumen macadam or concrete. BS 7188 gives requirements for impact resistant surfacing and BS 5696: Part 3 states that surfacing must extend 1.75 m beyond the equipment. The

Maximum Potential Free Fall Height (MPFFH) – which is the height from which children can fall from equipment without serious injury – must be specified when the surface is selected. If the playground has no equipment and is not used for games, there is much more choice:

● any of the bitumen macadam road surfaces with a base of MoT Type 1 fill;
● 100 mm of dry stone with tarmac skim coat;
● compacted dry stone with bitumen emulsion binder;
● compacted dry stone;
● compacted sand on geotextile layer.

Training areas

Surfaces for sports need to be constructed very carefully if sports players are to reach international or Olympic standards, and this means that these surfaces must be constructed by contractors who specialize in this work.

Plate 28   *A rubber tile impact absorbing surface laid under children's swings. This shows clearly the extent of the safety surfacing required. Surfacing and swings by SMP Playgrounds. (Photograph by courtesy of SMP Playgrounds.)*

Plate 29 *A safety tile surface being bolted down to a prepared base. Surfacing by SMP Playgrounds. (Photograph by courtesy of SMP Playgrounds.)*

Typical bases provided for specialist surfaces are:

- 100 mm of dry stone with tarmac skim coat;
- compacted dry stone with bitumen emulsion binder;
- compacted dry stone and geotextile layer;
- compacted sand with geotextile layer.

In any case the specialist sub-contractor will specify the type of base that is acceptable in order to guarantee the surface.

7.3 SUNK PATHS

These can be used in many ways to amuse, guide, or control pedestrians towards landscape features along a prescribed route. Examples of this kind of control are access to viewpoints, information boards, gateways and any point where it is undesirable that people should wander across grass or planted areas at will. They can also provide an entertaining indirect route, as in a maze or labyrinth, without the risk of losing the children in the undergrowth. Although sunk paths do not offer the same strength of crowd control as do fences, they will constrain most people without the visual obstruction caused by fences or walls (see Figure 7.2).

Sunk paths should be wide enough for wheelchairs, and for two people to pass unless the routes are deliberately designed as one-way systems. Passing bays are useful to accommodate groups passing each other. The level of the paths should be not less than 300 mm below ground level so that it is not too easy to step up, nor more than 500 mm below ground so that people can get out if needs be. If the design demands that the path should be sunk below head level to create an invisible access, then emergency exit steps or ramps should be provided at 30 m intervals or less, so that people do not feel trapped, since although a hedge can be planted on top of a low wall to raise the height, people cannot be expected to charge through it even in emergency.

Good drainage of the sunk path is essential, and the retaining walls to each side should be backed by fin drains which can also take the path run-off through gulleys under the walls if the level of the groundwater permits. The path must be provided with drainage channels and gulleys if it is hard-surfaced, or constructed of self-draining material such as grass concrete or granular paving. Remember to check the natural level of the water table in wet weather, otherwise the path may develop into a canoeing course. The retaining walls can be planted with rockery plants to soften the appearance, or if more screening is required the wall can be hedged to increase the total height; soft banking is not suitable as soil can be washed down onto the path. An alternative is to construct sloping sides of embankment types of grass concrete which appears less constricting than vertical walls, though the run-off will have to be taken by channels and gulleys to a surface water drainage system unless the path surface is very permeable.

7.4 ROOF GARDENS

Before starting the design of a roof garden the landscape designer must check with the architect that the roof structure is capable of carrying the very heavy loading of earth, trees, water features and marble planters. This load is much greater than most architects realize, and unless the building has been designed from the start for a roof garden, it is advisable to confine the 'landscape' design to thin paving and lightweight planters with low shrubs and climbers on light framing. Even a well-trained tree needs a fair amount of earth, and the combined weight of a tree in full leaf, wet earth and a substantial planter can run into many tonnes, all resting on one point. Remember that all loads on a building eventually have to finish up on the foundations, and if these are not designed to take additional unexpected roof loads, the roof garden is likely to find itself flourishing in the basement. As well as the load, the chief building requirements are that the roof structure must

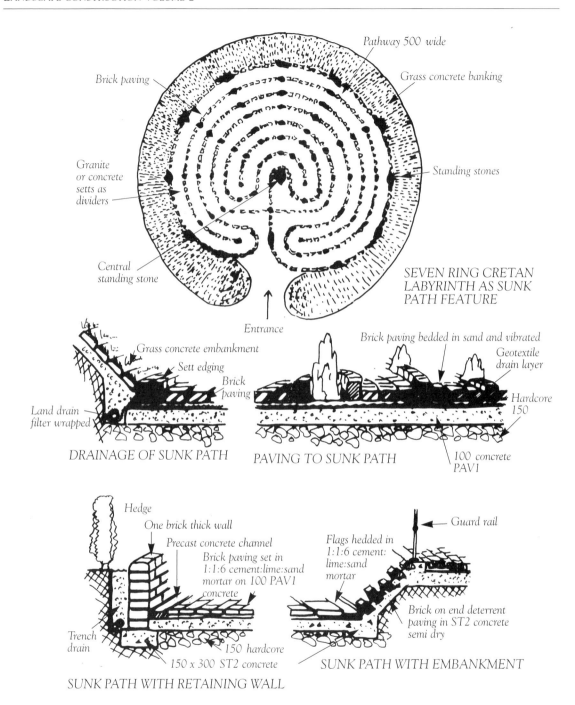

Pathway 500 wide

Brick paving

Grass concrete banking

Granite
or concrete
setts as
dividers

Standing stones

Central
standing stone

SEVEN RING CRETAN
LABYRINTH AS SUNK
PATH FEATURE

Entrance

Grass concrete embankment

Sett edging

Brick
paving

Land drain
filter wrapped

DRAINAGE OF SUNK PATH

Brick paving bedded in sand and vibrated

Geotextile
drain layer

Hardcore
150

100 concrete
PAV1

PAVING TO SUNK PATH

Hedge

One brick thick wall

Precast concrete channel

Brick paving set in
1:1:6 cement:lime:sand
mortar on 100 PAV1
concrete

Guard rail

Flags bedded in
1:1:6 cement:
lime:sand
mortar

Brick on end deterrent
paving in ST2 concrete
semi dry

Trench
drain

150 hardcore

150 x 300 ST2 concrete

SUNK PATH WITH EMBANKMENT

SUNK PATH WITH RETAINING WALL

Figure 7.2   Sunk Paths

withstand digging, root penetration, chemical attack from horticultural chemicals, and distortion due to uneven loading by landscape features (a pool will be full of water in summer and empty in winter, and a tree in full leaf weighs much more than a bare tree).

The combination of these factors means that the roof will probably need to be constructed of concrete with a concrete or brick upstand to contain the garden protected by tanking. A guard rail or other barrier is needed to stop people falling off the roof, and these guard railings can be concealed by an evergreen boundary hedge; in either case the barrier must comply with the Building Regulations. There should be as few projecting structures as possible, and they should be grouped into one or two enclosures to reduce the number of changes in the tanking. There are specialist firms who undertake roof garden tanking, and the landscape designer is advised to consult one of them in collaboration with the architect. An outline landscape plan will be needed to determine loading, and once the structure and tanking have been decided the landscape design can go ahead in the normal way.

Normal building roofs only have to resist rain and snow which can easily be drained off the surface, but roof planting will hold water over a considerable time, giving it the opportunity to cause leaks and corrosion. This means that the architect must provide a much higher standard of waterproofing – really tanking – to the roof, and the falls and drainage must have a greater capacity for removing water. Drainage water will probably have to run into the building drainage system, and the landscape designer should check that this is acceptable to the local authority.

The roof can be waterproofed by flexible butyl rubber sheeting, protected by concrete promenade tiles or aggregate, but this is rather unstable and also at risk from gardening tools; it is safer to tank the roof properly with mastic asphalt 30 mm thick in three-coat work as described in Chapter 2, Monolithic Paving, remembering that bitumen macadam or hot rolled asphalt are not suitable for high level work, as the introduction of a 5 tonne roller will cause a certain amount of consternation on site. The tanking should be laid on a cement:sand or lightweight concrete screed provided by the building contractor and laid to generous falls; 1 in 30 is a minimum. Drainage is the most important aspect of roof garden design, and a satisfactory solution is to lay perforated vitrified clay drainage tiles (such as those used in sewage works) on the tanking, cover them with a geotextile filter fabric which has a slow rate of percolation, and to spread the soil on top (see Figure 7.3). The soil must be at least 300 mm thick for grass, small shrubs and herbaceous planting, with more for large shrubs and trees, evenly structured, free-draining but capable of retaining moisture, and not likely to become dusty and blow off the roof. This may require the addition of water-holding granules or other binders to the soil. A good mulch of heavy bark chips on the soil will help to preserve the moisture, but any planting in such severe conditions must be very carefully maintained. A permanent piped irrigation and feeding system, controlled by a programmer, may be desirable for all but the smallest roof garden.

Hard paving in walkways can be sand bedded small unit flags, setts, or brick pavers laid on DoT granular material on the geotextile. Rigid cement mortar bedding is liable to movement in the extremes of temperature found on high roofs, and the movement of the building structure itself will have to be matched by corresponding movement joints in the hard paving. Flexible construction that can accommodate itself to the building movement is less liable to failure.

Large vegetation at a high level is susceptible to wind pressure far more than ground level planting, and the architect may have to provide wind-break walls or screens if mature trees are wanted. Such trees will have to be permanently anchored, and this means that the architect should provide fixing points in the main building structure, since ground anchors or stakes cannot be used. These fixing points need not be unsightly; a statue of a wood nymph leaning casually on a tree may really be supporting the tree by means of steel reinforcement down her spine. The shallow Amsterdam Tree Soil planting technique may be useful for large trees. It is as well to provide some open screening at the roof edges as well as safety barriers, since branches, gravel, or water spray can be blown over on to pedestrians or cars below. Even small stones can be very painful when coming down from 50 m or more. Roof gardens on very high buildings are better designed as enclosed structures with a completely artificial climate.

Water features are always attractive in a roof garden, but they must be easy to maintain and as foolproof as possible. Overflow arrangements for pools must be capabale of dealing with the flooding caused by heavy rainfall, jammed water pumps, or champagne bottles in the outlet, and simple weir overflows discharging into channels connected directly to the rainwater drainage system are probably the most satisfactory. These outlets must be screened to prevent leaves and rubbish from entering the rainwater downpipes.

7.5 ROAD HUMPS

Road humps are a recommended method of restraining traffic from travelling at speeds which are dangerous for the driver or the pedestrian and are much used on 'rat-runs' where fast commuter traffic can cause accidents. Their main use in landscape design is to check traffic at the entrance to car parks, school driveways, country parks, shopping centres and similar places where pedestrians and vehicles are likely to come into conflict. Road humps should not be used on bus routes – this could equally well apply to ambulances, buses for the disabled and disabled drivers' vehicles on private roads, as passengers can be thrown about if the vehicle goes too fast over the hump. Fire engines also cannot travel fast over humps. The location, size, profile and signposting of humps on public roads are very carefully controlled, and the landscape designer would be well advised to follow these details even though the controls do not apply to private roads. Humps which do not conform to Section 90e of the Highways Act 1990 may make the owner liable for damages in the event of an accident or damage to a driver or passenger, even if they are driving within the speed limit. Probably the best type of road hump for

Figure 7.4   Road humps

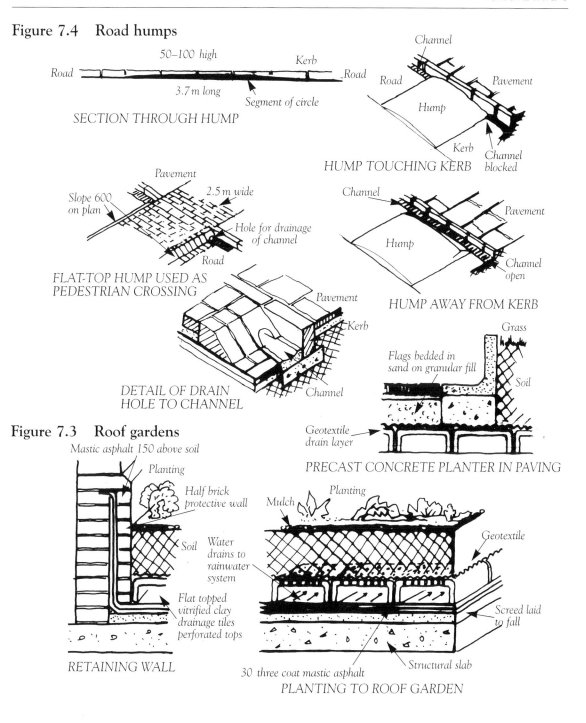

50–100 high

Road ——————————————— Road

Kerb

3.7 m long

Segment of circle

SECTION THROUGH HUMP

Channel

Road

Pavement

Hump

Kerb

Channel blocked

HUMP TOUCHING KERB

Pavement

Slope 600 on plan

2.5 m wide

Hole for drainage of channel

Road

FLAT-TOP HUMP USED AS PEDESTRIAN CROSSING

Channel

Pavement

Hump

Channel open

HUMP AWAY FROM KERB

Pavement

Kerb

DETAIL OF DRAIN HOLE TO CHANNEL

Channel

Grass

Flags bedded in sand on granular fill

Soil

Geotextile drain layer

PRECAST CONCRETE PLANTER IN PAVING

Figure 7.3   Roof gardens

Mastic asphalt 150 above soil

Planting

Half brick protective wall

Soil

Water drains to rainwater system

Flat topped vitrified clay drainage tiles perforated tops

RETAINING WALL

Mulch

Planting

Geotextile

Screed laid to fall

30 three coat mastic asphalt

Structural slab

PLANTING TO ROOF GARDEN

171

private roadways is the flat-topped hump which gives good warning to slow down without jerking the vehicle sharply; the flat top makes an excellent pedestrian crossing, as it can be made level with the footway. Typical road humps are shown in Figure 7.4. These humps consist of a ramp:

- rising 100 mm in 600 mm length, with a flat top of 2.5 m, then a descending ramp 600 mm long;
- rising 100 mm in 1000 mm length, with a flat top 3.6 m, then a descending ramp 1000 mm long.

They can be made of coloured blocks or marked with road-marking paints, and they must be signposted.

A possible future development is the use of 'speed cushions' which are small humps wide enough to force narrow vehicles to go over them with one wheel, but narrow enough to allow buses and emergency vehicles to straddle them. Bicycles can dodge them altogether. These cushions are about 2000 mm square, with a 1:8

Plate 30 *A flat-topped road hump which also forms an informal pedestrian crossing which is very suitable for prams and wheelchairs.*

slope for the traffic flow, and a 1:4 slope on the sides; they have a 800 mm platform on top, while a larger version is 2000 x 3700 mm long with a 2500 mm platform. The slopes are designed to slow down cars but not to upset cyclists.

7.6 ROADWAY MARKING

Roadways, playgrounds, and especially car parks, need to be marked out to control the traffic and to indicate special uses such as trolley bays, disabled parking areas and safety areas for play equipment. These markings are mostly made with hot-applied thermoplastic materials specified in BS 3262: Part 1. They are made of light coloured aggregate, pigment, and an extender bonded with thermoplastic resin which is applied hot from special machinery for permanent marking. The colours used usually are white and yellow, but others can be obtained. The landscape designer is advised to make quite sure that the markings are correctly shown on the drawings, as the smell and fumes caused by burning off errors are appalling, and faint confusing traces of the lines will always remain as a reproachful ghost.

7.7 MATERIALS FOR DECORATIVE SURFACING

Chippings
Chippings are sharp edged stone particles of even size, usually prepared from a strongly coloured natural stone, though artificially coloured material is available. Chippings can be had in ranges of sizes from 6 to 20 mm, and are equal sized within the range. They are best suited to grave surfacing, but they have a limited place in ornamental finish to planters and tree pits, where they are usually laid in a single layer 25–50 mm thick. Chippings are rather harsh in appearance, mostly made from the harder granite, marble and spar rocks which offer little roothold to algae and weeds as they stay clean with little maintenance.

Shingle
Shingle is composed of water rounded stones taken from river or sea beaches, or excavated from geologically old raised beaches. Beach or marine shingle should be washed. The winning of shingle in the UK is very strictly controlled by national and international legislation, and it is not a material to be selected by the landscape designer without proper consideration of environmental effects. Unfortunately, a good deal of shingle (and other ornamental stone) is imported from countries who care nothing for conservation, and the landscape designer should bear this in mind when specifying natural stone of any kind. Shingle is not suitable for paving as such, since it is very uncomfortable to walk on as any Brighton bather knows, but it has a use as a background material in planters or

ornamental tree surrounds to contrast with more formal paving. Loose shingle or cobbles should never be used in vandal-prone areas. Shingle comes in colours ranging from grey/white flints to rough warm sandstones and granites. Some types are:

- Scottish beach pebbles; mixed colours 30–50 mm
- white marble pebbles; bright white 25–40 mm
- quartz; white/pink/grey 25–45 mm
- water worn flints; grey/white/brown 20–30 mm

It is usually laid as a single layer of material, tapped lightly to consolidate it, and owing to its extremely open texture a geotextile membrane is essential to prevent the base material from mixing with it. Shingle may be one size or graded to form a more compact surface.

8 MAINTENANCE AND REPAIRS

Maintenance and repair of paving is an aspect of landscape design which should be of some concern to the designer, as much good paving has been spoilt by subsequent clumsy or indifferent repairs. Paving is subject to many types of damage; the most common of these are discussed in this section.

Vehicles

Vehicles going where they shouldn't and cracking the surface, and vehicles being heavier than those for which the paving was designed and cracking the surface and even the foundation of the paving.

Oil, petrol and spills from vehicles. People will park where they shouldn't, regardless of any prohibition, and somehow it always seems to be the dirtiest, leakiest and most disreputable car which parks on light buff brick paving. The only way to keep illegal parking at bay is to provide an immovable physical barrier to the paving.

Subsidence

Lifting or subsidence caused by tree roots. This is a type of damage which should be under the control of the landscape designer, but sometimes ill-advised planting takes place after the contract is finished, and rapidly growing trees can soon cause root damage to paving. Hidden roots from trees cut down long before the contract, but whose roots are still under the paving, can cause problems either because they eventually rot and cause subsidence or because they grow a fine crop of fungi which can lift even the largest paving flag.

Subsidence caused by inadequate inspection of the subsoil. The landscape designer is often presented with a layer of broken bricks, scrap timber and steel, and old rubber boots as the foundation for paving, and even when these are cleared away, weak areas of the subsoil may not be apparent. The whole area of the proposed paving should be examined for soft areas, drain lines, old foundations and other factors which would affect the level of the finished paving. It is worth checking old maps and local authority records in cases where a possibility of concealed underground structures and services exists, such as former industrial sites.

Subsidence and consequent ponding of rainwater (due to vehicle overrun or to specifying an inadequate base to the paving) which may cause frost damage to the surface.

Chemicals and abrasion

Erosion and damage by chemicals. If there is any likelihood of strong chemicals such as bleach or acid being spilt or stored on the paving, the landscape designer should check the performance of the proposed paving with the manufacturer. Modern epoxy resin surfaces are resistant to most things, as are the traditional granite setts, but the landscape designer should bear in mind that the more chemicals a paving material has to stand up to, the more expensive it will be.

Abrasion and scarring – this is likely to occur where heavy benches, tables, hand operated machinery, or pallets are dragged over the surface. Buildings where goods or equipment are frequently carried in and out, such as factories, schools, shops, craft workshops and public houses are the most likely to generate scarring traffic. Publicans in particular have deliveries of hard-edged kegs and crates, and frequently move picnic benches and tables about the site.

Repairs

Damage can be caused by incompetence or unavoidable difficulties in repairing the paving. The landscape designer may be surprised by the number of times someone is going to dig up the paving in the course of a few years. Paving may be lifted for repairs to soil drains, surface water drains, electricity lines, water services pipes, gas service pipes, telephone cables, and other underground services, as well as for the installation of any new services for buildings. Paving will also have to be lifted to repair damage caused by any of the factors listed above. There is a continuous but fairly amicable argument between those designers who prefer unit paving, as they maintain that it is easier to lay a number of small units which do not require hot or liquid material, and those designers who support the flexibility of monolithic paving repairs. In the landscape designer's ideal world, all those authorities and individuals responsible for unit paving maintenance would hold stocks of all types of unit paving in their area and would make sure that contractors were issued with the appropriate paving for each repair. What happens in practice is that the contractor uses the nearest paving to the original that can be obtained easily and cheaply, or else the repair is carried out with bituminous or concrete material. When unit paving is first laid, it may be vibrated mechanically to settle it firmly, and the same firmness cannot be obtained by hand vibration of small repairs. Unless great care over laying is taken, and good supervision of the work is specified, the unit paving must either be left proud to settle later, in which case people will trip over it, or laid level, when it will sink later and people will again trip over it.

It is certainly much easier to lay repair patches in monolithic paving, since bituminous or concrete materials are more standard than unit paving and therefore more likely to match the original surface. The monolithic patch can be smoothly graded to the existing, so that when settlement takes place there is no sharp edge to trip over.

Granular paving is probably the easiest to damage, but it is also the easiest to repair. It is especially liable to wear into ruts or pools, and any minor scuffle, scrape or impact will mark gravel or hoggin, but most damage can be made good by raking or infilling with fresh material. Weed control is also a problem, since the loose surface offers a foothold (or roothold) for invasive weeds, and weed control should be part of the planned maintenance programme. On the estates of the great houses, gravel was traditionally raked and levelled every day; each hoof-mark, leaf and weed being removed before it could leave any trace. Although such a programme is no longer feasible, modern weed control methods and regular regrading can keep granular surfaces in good condition for many years without the need to replace them. Granular paving is particularly suitable for absorbing spills, which can then be dug out and replaced with fresh material.

LIST OF BRITISH STANDARDS

Some of the Standards listed here are not covered in the main text; they are included here for those readers who wish to study the subjects in greater detail.

1.0 GENERAL

4428 : 1989 & AMD	Code of practice for general landscape operations
5930 : 1981	Code of Practice for site investigations

1.1 BASES

1377 : Pt 1: 1990	Methods of test for soils for engineering purposes: General requirements and sample preparation
1377 : Pt 2: 1990	Soil tests for civil engineering Classification requirements
1377 : Pt 4: 1990 & AMD	Soil tests for civil engineering Compaction related tests
1377 : Pt 5: 1990 & AMD	Soil tests for civil engineering Compressibility, permeability, durability
1377 : Pt 9: 1990 & AMD	Soil tests for civil engineering. In situ tests
5837 : 1991	Code of Practice for trees in relation to construction
6543 : 1985	Industrial by-products and waste materials: road making
8000 : Part 1: 1989	Workmanship on building sites. Part 1 Excavation and Filling

1.2 CONCRETE

882 : 1992 & AMD	Aggregates from natural sources for concrete
1881 : Pts 101–107, 114, 116	Methods of sampling fresh concrete on site
3892 : Pt 2: 1993	PFA for use in grouts and for miscellaneous uses in concrete
5075 : Pt 1: 1982 & AMD	Concrete admixtures: accelerating, retarding, and water reducing
5075 : Pt 2: 1982 & AMD	Concrete admixtures: air-entraining admixtures
5328 : Pt 1: 1991 & AMD	Guide to specifying concrete
5328 : Pt 2: 1991	Methods for specifying concrete
5328 : Pt 3: 1990	Methods for specifying concrete
5328 : Pt 4: 1990	Methods for specifying concrete
EN ISO 9001	Quality approval for Designated Mixes

2.1 MACADAM

63 : Pt 1: 1987	Single sized aggregate for general purposes
63 : Pt 2: 1987	Single sized aggregate for surface dressing
434 : Pt 1: 1984	Bitumen road emulsions
434 : Pt 2: 1984	Code of Practice for use of bitumen road emulsions
3690 : Pt 1: 1989	Bitumens for roads and other paved areas
4987 : Pt 1: 1993	Coated macadam for roads and other paved areas
4987 : Pt 2: 1993	Coated macadam for roads and other paved areas: transport, laying and compaction
6543 : 1985	Industrial by-products and waste materials: road making

2.2 ASPHALT

63 : Pt 1: 1987	Single sized aggregate for general purposes
63 : Pt 2: 1987	Single sized aggregate for surface dressing
434 : Pt 1: 1984	Bitumen road emulsions
594 : Pt 1: 1985	Hot rolled asphalt for roads and other paved areas
594 : Pt 2: 1992	Transport, laying, and compaction of hot rolled asphalt
3690 : Pt 1: 1989	Bitumens for roads and other paved areas
6044 : 1987	Pavement Marking Paints
6543 : 1985	Industrial by-products and waste materials: road making

2.3 MASTIC ASPHALT

63 : Pt 1: 1987	Single sized aggregate for general purposes
63 : Pt 2: 1987	Single sized aggregate for surface dressing
434 : Pt 1: 1984	Bitumen road emulsions
434 : Pt 2: 1984	Code of Practice for use of bitumen road emulsions
1446 : 1973	Mastic asphalt (natural rock) for roads and footways
1447 : 1988	Mastic asphalt (limestone) for roads, footways and paving in buildings
3690 : Pt 1: 1989	Bitumens for roads and other paved areas
6044 : 1987	Pavement Marking Paints
6543 : 1985	Industrial by-products and waste materials: road making

2.4 DENSE TAR SURFACES

63 : Pt 1: 1987	Single sized aggregate for general purposes
63 : Pt 2: 1987	Single sized aggregate for surface dressing
76 : 1994	Tars for road purposes
5273 : 1975	Dense tar surfacing for roads and other paved areas
6044 : 1987	Pavement Marking Paints
6543 : 1985	Industrial by-products and waste materials: road making

2.5 CONCRETE ROADS

882 : 1992 & AMD	Aggregates from natural sources for concrete
2499 : Pt 1: 1993	Hot-applied joint sealants for concrete pavements
3892 : Pt 2: 1993	PFA for use in grouts and for miscellaneous uses in concrete
4449 : 1988	Carbon steel bars for the reinforcement of concrete
4483 : 1985	Steel fabric for the reinforcement of concrete
5212 : Pt 1: 1990	Joint sealants for concrete pavements
5212 : Pt 2: 1990	Code of Practice for application and use of joint sealants for concrete pavements
5328 : Pt 1: 1991	Guide to specifying concrete
5328 : Pt 2: 1991	Methods for specifying concrete
5328 : Pt 3: 1990	Methods for specifying concrete
5328 : Pt 4: 1990	Methods for specifying concrete

3.1 FLAGS

882 : 1992 & AMD	Aggregates from natural sources for concrete
7263 : Pt 1: 1994	Precast concrete flags, kerbs, channels, edgings and quadrants
7263 : Pt 2: 1990	Code of Practice for laying precast concrete flags, kerbs, channels, edgings and quadrants

3.2 BLOCKS

882 : 1992 & AMD	Aggregates from natural sources for concrete
6677 : Pt 2: 1986	Code of Practice for the design of lightly trafficked pavements
6677 : Pt 3: 1986	Method of construction of pavements
6717 : Pt 1: 1993	Precast concrete paving blocks
6717 : Pt 3: 1989	Code of Practice for laying precast concrete paving blocks
7533 : 1992	Guide for structural design of pavements constructed with clay or concrete blocks

3.3 NATURAL STONE

435 : 1975	Dressed natural stone kerbs, channels, quadrants and setts

3.4 SETTS

PD 6472 : 1974	Guide to specifying the quality of building mortars
12 : 1991	Portland cement
882 : 1992 & AMD	Aggregates from natural sources for concrete
435 : 1975	Dressed natural stone setts
890 : 1972	Building limes
1200 : 1976 & AMD	Building sands from natural sources Sands for mortar for brickwork
6717 : Pt 1: 1993	Precast concrete paving blocks

3.5 BRICKS

PD 6472 : 1974	Guide to specifying the quality of building mortars
12 : 1991	Portland cement
187 : 1978 & AMD	Calcium silicate (flint/lime and sand/lime) bricks

882 : 1992 & AMD	Aggregates from natural sources for concrete
890 : 1972	Building limes
1200 : 1976 & AMD	Building sands from natural sources. Sands for mortar for brickwork
3921 : 1985	Clay bricks and blocks
4254 : 1983 (obsolescent)	Two-part polysulphide based sealants
4721 : 1981 (1986) & AMD	Ready mixed building mortars
4729 : 1990	Shapes and dimensions of special bricks
4887 : Pt 1: 1986	Mortar admixtures. Air-entraining (plasticizing) admixtures
4887 : Pt 2: 1987	Mortar admixtures. Set retarding admixtures
5889 : 1989 (obsolescent)	One-part gun-grade polysulphide sealants
6677 : Pt 1: 1986	Clay and calcium silicate pavers for flexible paving
6677 : Pt 2: 1986	Code of Practice for the design of lightly trafficked pavements
6677 : Pt 3: 1986	Method of construction of pavements

3.6 COBBLES
No British Standards apply directly to this subject.

3.7 GRASS CONCRETE
No British Standards apply directly to this subject.

3.8 DETERRENT PAVING
No British Standards apply directly to this subject.

4.1 GRAVEL
No British Standards apply directly to this subject.

4.2 BALLAST
No British Standards apply directly to this subject.

4.3 BARK
No British Standards apply directly to this subject.

5.0 – 5.2 KERBS AND EDGINGS

435 : 1975	Dressed natural stone kerbs, channels, quadrants and setts

| 7263 : Pt 1: 1994 | Precast concrete flags, kerbs, channels, edgings and quadrants |
| 7263 : Pt 2: 1990 | Code of Practice for laying precast concrete flags, kerbs, channels, edgings and quadrants |

5.3 MOWING STONES

| 435 : 1975 | Dressed natural stone kerbs, channels, quadrants and setts |
| 7263 : Pt 1: 1994 | Precast concrete flags, kerbs, channels, edgings and quadrants |

5.4 TREE GRILLES

3921 : 1985	Clay bricks and blocks
5837 : 1991	Code of Practice for trees in relation to construction
6717 : Pt 1: 1993	Precast concrete paving blocks
6717 : Pt 3: 1989	Code of Practice for laying precast concrete paving blocks

6.1 CHANNELS

435 : 1975	Dressed natural stone kerbs, channels, quadrants and setts
7263 : Pt 1: 1994	Precast concrete flags, kerbs, channels, edgings and quadrants
7263 : Pt 2: 1990	Code of Practice for laying precast concrete flags, kerbs, channels, edgings and quadrants

6.2 SURFACE WATER DRAINS

EN 124 : 1994 & AMD	Manhole covers, road gully gratings and frames for drainage purposes (replaces BS EN124: 1986 & BS 497: Pt1: 1976)
EN 295–5 : 1994	Vitrified clay pipes and fittings
EN 598 : 1995	Ductile iron pipes and fittings for sewerage (replaces 4772 : 1988)
65 : 1991 & AMD	Vitrified clay drain and sewer pipes
437 : 1978 & AMD	Cast iron spigot and socket drain pipes and fittings
1247 : Pt 1: 1990	Manhole step irons
4660 : 1989	PVC–U underground drain pipes and fittings 110 & 160 mm

5911 : Pt 2: 1982	Inspection chambers and street gulleys
5911 : Pt 100: 1988 & AMD	Unreinforced and reinforced concrete pipes and fittings with flexible joints
5911 : Pt 103: 1994	Precast concrete pipes: pre-stressed non-pressure pipes and fittings: flexible joints
5911 : Pt 110: 1992	Ogee jointed precast concrete pipes, bends and junctions, reinforced or unreinforced
5911 : Pt 114: 1992	Precast concrete porous pipes
5911 : Pt 120: 1989	Precast concrete pipes; reinforced jacking pipes with flexible joints
5911 : Pt 200: 1994	Precast concrete pipes: unreinforced and reinforced circular manholes and soakaways
5911 : Pt 230: 1994	Precast concrete inspection chambers and gulleys
5955 : Pt 6: 1980 & AMD	Code of Practice for installation of unplasticised PVC–U pipework for gravity drains and sewers
6180 : 1995	Code of Practice for protective barriers in and about buildings
6367 : 1983	Code of Pratice for drainage of roofs and paved areas
6437 : 1984 & AMD	Polyethylene pipes (type 50) in metric diameters for general purposes
7158 : 1989	Plastics inspection chambers for drains
8000 : Pt 14: 1989	Code of Practice for below ground drainage
8301 : 1985 AMD	Code of Practice for building drainage: including design and construction of ground water drains

6.3 LAND DRAINS

EN 295–5 : 1994	Vitrified clay pipes and fittings
1196 : 1989	Clayware field drain pipes and junctions
4962 : 1989	Plastics pipes and fittings for use as sub-soil field drains
5911 : Pt 101: 1988	Glass composite concrete (GCC) pipes and fittings with flexible joints
5911 : Pt 114: 1992	Precast concrete porous pipes
5911 : Pt 200: 1989	Precast concrete manholes, soakaways of circular cross section

7.1 DISABLED USERS
British Standards apply to individual materials and components.

7.2 PLAYGROUNDS AND SPORTS AREAS

5696 : Pt 2: 1986 & AMD	Playground equipment intended for permanent installation outdoors: specification for construction and performance
5696 : Pt 3: 1979 & AMD	Play equipment: Code of Practice for installation and maintenance
7044 : Pt 1: 1990	Artificial Sports Surfaces: classification, general introduction
7044 : Pt 2: S.2.5: 1990	Artificial Sports Surfaces: miscellaneous
7044 : Pt 4: 1991	Surfaces for multi-sports use. Gives requirements for artificial sports surfaces
7188 : 1989 & AMD	Testing impact absorbing playground surfaces

7.3 SUNK PATHS
British Standards apply to materials used in sunk paths.

7.4 ROOF GARDENS
No British Standards apply directly to this subject, but roof gardens are subject to the Building Regulations and therefore to the British Standards referred to therein.

7.5 ROAD HUMPS
No British Standards apply directly to this subject, but they are controlled by the Highways (Road Humps) Regulations 1990 SI 1990/703 and the Highways (Road Humps) (Amendment) Regulations 1990 SI 1990/1500.

7.6 ROAD MARKING

873 : Pt 4: 1987	Road studs
3262 : Pt 1: 1989	Hot applied thermoplastic road-marking materials
3262 : Pt 2: 1989	Hot applied thermoplastic road-marking materials: road performance
3262 : Pt 3: 1989	Hot applied thermoplastic road-marking materials: road surfaces

8.0 DECORATIVE FINISHES
British Standards are relevant to the material being used.

9.0 MAINTENANCE

7370 : Pts 1 and 2: 1991	Grounds Maintenance

GLOSSARY OF TERMS USED IN LANDSCAPE CONSTRUCTION (ROADS, PAVING AND DRAINAGE)

Accelerator	Chemical additive to concrete and mortar to speed up setting
Aggregate	Broken stone, natural pebbles or other hard material used for concrete, macadam roadways, etc.
Agricultural drain	Porous or perforated pipes for draining fields and soft landscape areas
Backfill	The material used to fill trenches after pipes have been laid
Ballast	A mixture of sand and gravel as dug from the pit
Basket weave	Bricks or blocks laid with two headers and a stretcher repeated to form a pattern similar to woven wickerwork
Battered	Sloping as in a retaining wall or one face of a kerb
Bedding	The operation of setting the paving units firmly on the base in sand or mortar, or the material used
Blinding	Fine layer of sand or ash spread on the sub-strate to fill large voids in the material
Blocks	Small precast concrete units usually bedded in sand and tightly locked together by vibration

Brick-on-edge	Bricks laid with the narrow long face uppermost
Brick-on-end	Bricks laid with the short face uppermost and the narrow long face outwards
Bull-nosed	A brick or block with one edge of the header rounded off: double bull-nose has two edges rounded off
Butt jointed	Laid very closely together with little or no joint
Camber	The fall from the centre of a road or paving to each side
CBR	California Bearing Ratio: the expected loading on a road given as a percentage; a higher percentage gives a better bearing ratio
Capping layer	A layer of hardcore laid on a doubtful sub-strate to form a sound foundation for the sub-base
Carpet	Slang name for the wearing surface of a macadam road
Catchwater drain	Trench filled with rubble or special aggregate to drain water from fields and alongside paths and roads
Cement bound macadam	Macadam bound with Portland cement mortar
Chamfered	Edges slightly splayed to prevent upstanding sharp edges from tripping people and also to stop the edges from getting chipped
Channel	Narrow sunk paving at the edge of the path or road which carries the run-off to a gulley
Chippings	Brightly coloured broken stone used for decorative finishes to planted areas or ornamental features
Cobbles	Naturally rounded stones shaped by present or geologically ancient water action
Cross-fall	The fall across a path or road from one side to the other
Culvert	A large pipe passing under a road or gateway to carry surface water; often used to enclose streams where open water could be dangerous
Dished	Shallow curved sinking in a gulley or channel
DoT Type Granular fill	Specifically graded aggregate which compacts to form a strong sub-base for paving or drains. Type 1 fill restricts the materials which can be included, Type 2 is more lax about the suitable materials
DPC	Damp Proof Course: a layer of impervious material in a wall or paving to prevent the transmission of moisture
Dropper kerb	A kerb which makes the transition between one kerb profile and another. Used at pavement crossings
Dry bound macadam	40 mm aggregate with fine material vibrated into it
DTS	Dense Tar Surfacing; a mixture of road tar, aggregate and filler used where oil spillage is a problem
Edge restraint	Generic term for kerb-like units used to stop block paving from spreading when it is vibrated

Edgings	Light precast concrete, timber or stone units laid to separate two different kinds of paving
Engineering bricks	Heavy dense clay bricks of very precise dimensions which were traditionally used for building railway and canal structures
Fall	The slope of a road or paving which allows water to drain off properly
Field drain	Porous or perforated pipes for draining fields and soft landscape areas
Filter fabric	Earlier name for geotextile material
Filter-wrapped	Pipe wrapped with geotextile fabric to prevent fine particles of soil from entering the pipe
Fin drain	Trench filled with aggregate, geotextile fabric and pipes to drain water from fields and alongside paths and roads
Fine picked	Close textured finish for granite
Fire paths	Special hard surfaces adjoining buildings where there is no road, used in emergency by fire engines
Flags	Paving units, usually precast concrete, up to 70 mm thick and up to 900 mm wide
Flame texturing	Passing a natural stone through a fierce flame to give it a crystalline finish which is less slippery
Flexible paving	Oddly enough, made of small rigid units such as bricks or blocks, but set in a soft sand bed as opposed to a solid concrete bed
Formation level	The natural or improved ground level on which the paving is formed
French drain	Trench filled with rubble or special aggregate to drain water from fields and alongside paths and roads
Geotextile	Flexible cloth material used to prevent mud or sand from oozing into clean gravel, hardcore or drain pipes
Granular material	Carefully graded aggregate (usually to DoT standards) used for sub-bases and pipe bedding
Granular paving	Generic name for loose materials such as gravel, bark, or ballast
Grass concrete	Precast concrete or plastic units with slots or holes which are sown with grass
Gravel	Particles ranging from 5 to 15 mm, consisting of crushed hard rock or natural pebbles
Half-brick thick	102.5 mm = half the length of a brick laid as a header
Hardcore	Clean dry broken brick, stone, or concrete from old buildings or brick and stone yards which is used as a firm hard base for concrete and other paving slabs; it must be free of dust, chemicals, oil, organic matter, and old rubber boots

Haunching	Cement or concrete backing to kerbs to steady them
Headers	Bricks or blocks laid with the short face showing
Herbicide	Weedkiller which destroys all vegetation
Herring-bone	Bricks or blocks laid at right angles to form a regular V-pattern
Hoggin	A naturally occurring material composed of well graded gravel in a clay matrix
Interceptor chamber	The last chamber in a private drain before the public sewer is reached. It has a trap which prevents smells, rats and foul air from coming back into the private drain
Invert	The level at the inside bottom of a pipe or drain
JCB	The all-purpose digger which does everything on the site; besides digging it can be seen carrying tea, unloading bricks, or nibbling away at old foundations
Jointing	Filling the gaps between paving units, either as they are laid, or afterwards, when it is called pointing
Kerb	The hard (usually slip-resistant) edge laid between two different surfaces such as pavements and roads
Kerb check	The part of the kerb which projects above the road or paving
Land drain	Porous or perforated pipes for draining fields and soft landscape areas
Manhole	Common term for any underground chamber giving access to drains or other services
Maul	Or beetle. A heavy wooden mallet or log with handles used for tapping paving units into place. It does not chip the stone as does a steel hammer
Mole drain	Land drain formed by pulling a special plough through the ground to form a tunnel in the soil
Monolithic	Paving or roadway laid as a continuous sheet, usually semi-liquid macadam or concrete
Mowing stone	Narrow strip of stone, brick or precast concrete alongside a wall or building to allow the mower to cut close up the structure
MPFFH	Maximum Potential Free Fall Height, which is the height from which children can fall from equipment without serious injury
Nidged	Medium textured finish for granite
One brick thick	215 mm = the length of a brick. Two 102.5 mm half bricks plus one 10 mm mortar joint = one brick
One-and-a-half-brick	327.5 mm = one 215 mm brick plus one 102.5 mm half brick plus one 10 mm mortar joint = 327.5 mm
Outfall	Point at which surface water is discharged into a ditch or stream

Pavers	Clay or concrete paving units thinner than standard bricks and designed to withstand hard wear
Paviour	The craftsman who lays paving. 'Pavers' and 'Paviours' are sometimes incorrectly interchanged
Pea gravel	Naturally occurring gravel with nearly all the stones the size of dried peas
Pedestrian deterrent	Very rough or uneven paving which is very difficult to walk or drive on
Pervious surface	Allows water to drain through the top layer of the road to an impervious layer beneath
PFA	Pulverized Fuel Ash: the waste product from coal-fired generating plant and other industries; used as a mix in concrete to make it denser, less permeable and more chemical resistant
Planter	Raised pre-fabricated or in situ container for plants, larger than a pot or tub
Plasticizers	Chemical additive to concrete and mortar to make them more workable when stiff or in cold weather
Quarry sap	The natural moisture present in freshly quarried stone
Quarry waste	Broken stone fragments from the quarry used for filling
Ponding	The collection of water on paving caused by blockage of the drainage system or bad drainage design
Random paving	Also known as 'crazy paving'; irregular shaped pieces of stone or broken concrete flags
Rapid-hardening	Chemical additive to cement to reduce the time before the concrete can be loaded
Regulating course	One of the macadam or asphalt road layers used to regulate the final road levels
Retarder	Chemical additive to concrete and mortar to extend the setting time so that larger amounts can be mixed at one time; used extensively for ready-mixed concrete and mortar which must travel to the site from some distance
Rigid paving	Hard paving units set in rigid concrete
Road base	The structural layer of a road immediately above the sub-base
Road formers	Reusable steel strips made to various profiles which hold the road material in position until it has set
Rodding eye	Small access point with a cover used for cleaning drains where a manhole is not available
Rough punched	Coarse textured finish for granite
Rubble drain	A simple trench filled with rubble to form a land drain
Sand-slitting	Cutting slots in waterlogged turf and filling them with grit or sand to improve the drainage

Sealant	Any soft putty-like material used for sealing gaps in paving or roads; they are applied hot or cold
Setts	Originally small brick-sized granite blocks used for paving heavily trafficked roads; now applies to precast concrete units
Shale	Mine waste
Sidefill	The material packed round the side of pipes in a trench
Sight lines	Statutory lines of sight at road junctions to enable drivers to see approaching traffic and pedestrians
Silt pit	Gulley with a specially deep bottom and a bucket which traps the silt and can be lifted out for cleaning
Single axed	Medium textured finish for granite
Slabs	Interchangeable with 'flags' but used in this book to denote natural stone paving
Soakaway	Brick or concrete pit in which surface water is collected to allow it to disperse gradually into the surrounding soil
Spalling	Flakes split off from stone or brick by the action of frost
Squint	Angled or crooked. A squint arch goes through a wall at an angle, not straight through
Stable pavers	Traditional hard clay pavers with chequered surfaces used in stables to give horses a good grip
Stack bond	Bricks or blocks laid side by side with all joints straight through
Stretchers	Bricks or blocks laid with the long face showing
Sub-base	The most important layer of the road construction; the design of the sub-base is critical to the overall strength of the road
Sub-strate or sub-grade	The natural ground level on which the paving or road is constructed
Sulphate resisting	Cement which has the ability to withstand chemical attack from sulphates in the soil
Sur-bedded	Natural stone laid the wrong way up, with the natural planes of the stone vertical instead of horizontal
Sward	Traditional name for well-established close grown turf
Tactile flag	Precast concrete flag with a pattern of raised dots on it used to identify crossings for blind people
Tamping	Consolidating a surface by banging the edge of a plank gently on it till a given level is reached
Tanking	Not really to do with tanks as such – the layer of waterproof material applied to a wall, roof or floor to make it completely watertight
Tree grille	Or grid: open slotted iron, concrete, brick or timber frame around a tree in hard paving to allow water to reach the tree

Trench soakaway	Long soakaway following the ground contours
Unit paving	Paving made of small square or rectangular bricks, stones, or concrete laid individually or by special machines
Water-bound macadam	Macadam bound with sand and water
Weir kerb	Special kerb with holes leading water from the channel to a drain behind the kerb. Used where gulleys in the channel are not desirable
Wet lean concrete	Concrete with less than the normal amount of cement
Wet-mix macadam	40 mm aggregate bound with bituminous material

BIBLIOGRAPHY OF BOOKS RELEVANT TO LANDSCAPE CONSTRUCTION (ROADS, PAVING AND DRAINAGE)

Ashurst, J. and N. (1988), *Practical Building Conservation Vol I, II, III*, Aldershot, Gower.

Beazley, E. (1960), *Design and Detail of the Space between Buildings*, 1st ed., London, Architectural Press.

Brick Development Association, *Flexible Brick paving: application and design*.

British Aggregate Construction Materials Industries, *What's in a Road* and *Roads and footways on housing estates*.

British Cement Association, *Cement-bound materials for sub-bases and road bases*.

British Clayware Land Drain Industry, *Guide to land drains*.

Cutler, D.F., and Richardson, I.D.K. (1989), *Tree Roots and Buildings*, 2nd ed., London, Construction Press.

Department of the Environment, *Residential roads and footpaths*.

Department of Transport, *Notes for guidance on the Specification for Highway Works* and *Use of dropped kerbs and tactile surfaces at pedestrian crossing points*

Interpave, Concrete Block Paving Association, various useful publications.

Legislation:
Building Regulations England and Wales (current issue)
   Approved Document C *Site preparation and resistance to moisture*
                    H *Drainage and waste disposal*

K *Stairs, ramps and guards*
M *Access and facilities for disabled people*
Highways (Road Humps) Regulations 1990; SI 1990/703 (and Amendments).
Highways (Traffic Calming) Regulations 1993; SI 1993/1849.
Mastic Asphalt Council and Employers Federation Ltd, *Paving Handbook*.

Most trade associations publish useful technical guidance in conjunction with their product catalogues.

INDEX